MURDER AT THE
MANSARD HOUSE

Murder at the Mansard House

A DETECTIVE DAVID MACDONALD MURDER MYSTERY

Jane E Mengesha

This novel is a work of fiction. The names, characters and events are all from the writer's imagination. Any resemblance to persons, places and or events is coincidental. Some of the locations and establishments do exist and are used fictionally only as part of the settings.

ISBN: 1516929055
ISBN 13: 9781516929054

This novel is dedicated to my mother, Emily Mackin. (In Memoriam)

PROLOGUE

Lilian arrived earlier than usual that Monday morning. All seemed well at the Mansard House, the nursing home where she worked. When she entered the double doors, security reminded her it was street-cleaning day and to park only on the left side of the street. *This place*, Lilian thought. *Don't they realize we need more parking?* Her day started with the usual routine, checking e-mails, getting coffee, and returning calls.

Lilian was a busy physician's assistant, which meant that her job required that she covered shifts for a few doctors, and she had quite a few residents who needed to see her yesterday. After her midday report, Lilian called her friend Jenn to plan their lunch rendezvous. Taking a proper lunch break was important to both of them. They had become fast friends and enjoyed giggling about family events, recipes, and their plans for the weekend.

The other departments were all busy with their duties, as were the nurses, caring for their patients. The yearly State survey for regulatory compliance was due soon. Everything was being checked for compliance so they were survey-ready. Lilian enjoyed her position at the Mansard House. She worked hard to become a physician's assistant and felt her position was a blessing. The nursing staff cared for her and valued her loving way with the patients and her affectionate manner.

The nursing director, Minnie McCracken, was a pleasant, organized, and self-directed individual. She was very interactive with her staff, and their concerns were her concerns.

The administrator, Father Michael, was a quiet man and ran the Mansard with the budget in mind, as most administrators did. His constant reflection was his greatest asset in understanding the needs of his staff. He was often on morning rounds, making sure the residents' needs were met, the halls were neat and clean, and there was nothing out of order.

Father Pat, head nurse for Mansard 6, was assisting with the men's feeding group when Father Michael walked by. He nodded to him as Father Michael was bending over to pick up a wrapper off the floor. The start of the day appeared to be business as usual, but something felt amiss. Father Michael couldn't quite put his finger on it. The clouds started turning gray. Rain was in the forecast. Employees continued to arrive at work and punch in to start their day.

The housekeepers were in very early to start mopping and polishing floors and distributing laundry. The kitchen staff was busy preparing for the day's meals. The smell of baked bread and bacon filled the corridors leading out of the kitchen. Father checked his watch. *Almost time for breakfast*, he thought.

Father Michael greeted his staff. He expected them to do their best for the residents at all times. He often said that's why they were there. It was the mission of the order to feed the hungry, clothe the poor, and care for the sick. Father Michael spotted Lilian in the hallway, near the cafe.

"Good morning, Lilian. Don't forget about our meeting tomorrow. We will need the update on, the medical diagnosis codes for June. Everyone will need to be aware of these changes, as they will affect our reimbursement," Father said.

"Of course, Father. I'm well prepared," she said.

"Very well, dear, I'll let you on your way then."

With a nod, he continued on his rounds. Lilian rolled her eyes as he walked off out of sight. She sighed. *As if I didn't have enough to do. Oh well*, she thought as she scurried to do her next task. She was grateful to have a secure job with all the layoffs and cutbacks occurring in health care.

Suddenly the code alert alarmed. *Code 2! Code 2!* Rehab unit. Emergency personnel flew to the scene, including Father Michael. The residents were crying, nurses were barking orders.

"Grab the crash cart!" the head nurse yelled.

There lay a grim discovery. In the resident's room, a visiting priest from an affiliate order was found face down in a pool of blood. The head nurse checked for a pulse, but there was none. Father Michael was shocked. He recognized Father Don immediately. *Oh my God*, he thought. *Remain calm*. It first appeared that he might have fallen and lacerated his head, but no sooner had that thought entered Father Michael's mind when he noticed the sunlight peeking through the blinds and reflecting on a shiny object under the commode in the resident's room. He turned his attention to a crying patient.

When he turned back to the scene, the Swiss Army knife that he noticed a moment ago was no longer there. He suddenly felt sick to his stomach. "Please stand back and move away from the room, everyone. Return the residents to their rooms and close all the doors till this is over," he said.

Lilian was entering the unit just as the Boston Police arrived. She could hear the murmurings of the other residents and staff as police officers blocked off the area with yellow caution tape. The coroner's office was called, and the body was removed from the room and placed in the holding morgue.

"This is now a crime scene. Father Michael, please evacuate the area and remain calm," a police officer stated. "Do not let anyone enter this room."

Father Michael looked at the officer.

"It may have been an unfortunate accident," Father Michael said.

"We will soon know for sure," the officer replied. "There will be a full investigation as we determine the exact cause of death. Please do your best to control your staff. Oh, and Father, no one leaves the building for the time being."

With all the commotion, no one noticed the young visitor leaving the floor and escaping through the fire escape, down through the rusted stairs into the back alley, where the dumpsters were stored.

Quietly unlocking the gate, she casually and quickly walked across West Broadway, unnoticed.

CHAPTER 1

FATHER MICHAEL KNEW what this meant. If someone had murdered Father Don, what could have been the reason? This question rattled his brain. He walked down the front steps and into his car. He took his time driving to Castle Island. It was a windy day, and he needed a walk around the island to clear his head. It had been many years since he'd thought about his home in Killorglin, and he dreamed of the day he could return to the family he left behind. South Boston was a close reminder of his homeland, but nowhere could replace his birthplace. Driving along the water, Father thought about his journey long ago that had brought him to this place.

He hadn't always been a priest. In the early 1970s, he was a young physician working in Ethiopia with famine relief. Many Irish volunteers worked there with famine relief, as they were sympathetic to the pain and suffering so similar to what their own people had endured.

He parked his car and buttoned his coat to keep out the blustering wind. The ocean in the harbor was busting up the shoreline. Trees swayed with the strong winds. He passed the monument of the firefighter, lost in the line of duty, and took a seat to look out over the ocean.

The sound of the waves had a calming effect on him. He recalled his spiritual awakening. It had happened while he was volunteering in Ethiopia in one of the refugee camps.

He felt it overwhelm him, a calling, just like Saint Luke, as portrayed in Taylor Caldwell's *Dear and Glorious Physician*. That's how he described it. He'd known, of course, his life would change from that moment forward.

In Ethiopia his true calling to feed the hungry, clothe the poor, and heal the sick occurred daily. These poor people, he had thought. How much can they suffer?

He thought of his late wife, Marie, a clinic nurse for Save the Children in the outskirts of Addis Ababa, the country's capital. Medical care was needed there. The farm people traveled many miles to carry their sick family members, even those near death, to the free clinic for any and every treatment. Antibiotic supplies were limited, and oftentimes shipments of supplies were never distributed, as social welfare was secondary to the political unrest and bands of thieves. He thought of Marie and her kindness to the children, often staying up all night to minister to them as they lay dying. Malaria and, yes, AIDS were serious and deadly.

A cold wind, thunderclap, and rain brought Father Michael back to the present. It started to storm. He ran to Mulligan's, a local take-out restaurant, and stood under the awning till the rain subsided. He went in for coffee and a frankfurter and settled into a back corner to enjoy his meal.

He did not want to be disturbed. While sitting, he saw a police cruiser and homicide unit park out front. Moments later, Detective David MacDonald introduced himself.

"Father, I'm sorry to disturb you, but we need you to come down to the station while we file our report."

"Detective, do you mind if we have a quick smoke before we go?" Father Michael asked..

"Father, I'm surprised you smoke," said the detective.

"What, did you think that priests were perfect?" Father replied.

With a chuckle, Detective MacDonald offered him a Camel. "You could have fooled me, Father." He smiled.

The Boston Police Headquarters was located in downtown Boston.. Detective MacDonald questioned him for a little under an hour regarding the victim, Father Donald Ray O'Sullivan. Father Michael finally had to admit that they'd gone to seminary school together. "Withholding information in a murder investigation is paramount to obstruction of justice," the detective informed him. "Father, you need to retain an attorney."

"Detective, are you saying I am a suspect? That's ridiculous. I'm devastated by what's happened."He said.

"Father, again, I would recommend that you not say anything until you have an attorney present," the detective replied. "Remember, you cannot leave town for any reason," he added.

"What about a walk to Dorchester Heights? Are you going to arrest me for that?"

"Father, there is no need to get upset. Please return to your home and do as I say.

We will be in touch."

The funeral for Father Donald O'Sullivan was at the Nolan Funeral Home. The street was lined on both sides, as he had been the pastor for many years at St George's Church in Dorchester and was well loved in the community. Detective MacDonald attended the service as well. He was amazed at the turnout and gave his condolences to the family. He still could not understand what the motive could have been behind murdering a priest while visiting an elderly parishioner. MacDonald tipped his hat at Father Michael as he strolled toward the square on his way to the local pub on the corner.

You see, Detective MacDonald knew the neighborhood, too. He lived not too far from the church and had grown up down the street. He could see the church from the bar and watched as the mourners strayed outside and headed to their cars for the funeral procession. Some of the nurses that worked at the Mansard were there as well. Out of the corner of his eye, he could see across the street to the old high school. The road to the entrance of Dorchester Park was there. He focused his vision and could see a shadow of a woman behind a tree watching the procession of cars and relatives leaving the church. He thought to himself, *why does she look familiar? Where have I seen that silhouette before?* He returned to nursing his beer, but the shadow of that figure lurked under the surface of his scally cap.

CHAPTER 2

ZIGGY WORKED ON the rehab unit four days a week. Occasionally she would cover one of the long-term care units. Mr. Darcy was one of her favorite patients. He was a funny, quirky man with a good sense of humor and a kind heart. They often had long talks about her homeland and her life in the countryside of Ethiopia and her life in the United States now.

Ziggy lived in a rooming house in Chelsea with other Ethiopians, just struggling trying to make ends meet. She could only afford this lifestyle for the time being and someday hoped to buy her own home. Her dream was to eventually bring her brother and sister to come and live with her. Their parents were killed during an uprising in Ethiopia and the young ones remained in a UN refugee camp in Kenya. Ziggy and her siblings walked by nightfall to reach the refugee camp across the border. They hid during the day and traveled at night when it was safer. It took them five days to make it to the refugee camp in Kenya.

Father Don sponsored her to come to this country through the International Aid organization in Kenya. Ziggy was very sad Father Don was gone. He was such a support to her and others that had emigrated from third-world countries. The last time she saw him, she gave him a beautiful treasure of a gold-plated, framed portrait of Madonna and child.

Ziggy was not happy with Mr. Darcy's family. The oldest son, Tom, was just a mean-spirited man. The daughter, Crystal, was a selfish girl, basically waiting for her father to die.

Crystal acted very loving, but when no one was in the room, she would ignore her father and check her messages on her cell phone. She rarely visited and when she did, all she did was complain to the staff. "My father doesn't like his roommate, the food is lousy here, and why isn't he getting physical therapy today?" she would say. The nurses on the floor were often in the room, trying to appease the family. Mr. Darcy himself rarely had a complaint. Oftentimes he was confused and would call out to his late wife, Margaret. Margaret died a few months earlier, but the family decided not to let him know since his confusion would get worse and they felt it would only make him upset.

Ziggy didn't like to be around his family. They were always accusing her of this and that. Sometimes she would pretend she didn't understand English that well, when in fact she could understand very well. She knew his family was up to no good and wanted to blame everyone but themselves for their father's condition. When Mr. Darcy entered the Mansard, he was twenty pounds underweight, had bedsores, and was dehydrated. His physical health improved since his admission, but his mental health was deteriorating.

Ziggy was at the home the day Father Don was murdered. She saw the Swiss Army knife under the commode and took it before she left the building. She knew it was Father Michael's knife and wondered how it got there and who did this to her Father Don. She didn't care about obstructing justice. What did that mean to her? Not much, coming from a country where there was constant obstruction of justice. She knew in her heart that Father Don would not want Father Michael, his dear friend, involved or implicated in his death. Ziggy had other suspicions in her mind. She knew there were evil people in the world who would stop at nothing for money. Money and power were almost always motives in her mind. She was suspicious of Mr. Darcy's children. He was very wealthy and she knew they were waiting for him to die, to get his inheritance.

Ziggy finished up her duties for the day and headed home toward Chelsea, but not before stopping at the Awasa Restaurant to pick up her supper. She enjoyed visiting the restaurant and chatting with others from her country, speaking easily in her native tongue. It was tiring for her to always speak English. The food was similar to her mother's cooking. She waited awhile on the bar stool and drank a small glass of *tej(beer)* while she relaxed. Soon her *doro wat* (stew) was ready. She ordered an extra side of *injera* (bread)to share with some of her roommates.

Ziggy kept her part of the apartment very neat. The other roommates were a little sloppy, and she was a bit resentful, frequently turning off the lights and picking up after them. Father Michael allowed her to stay in the nursing home when she first arrived in this country. He was very kind to her. It took her about a year to find a place to live and time to get certified as a nursing assistant. She was forever grateful to him.

Ziggy thought of the funeral. She was so upset; she could only observe the service from afar. She did not want people to know her business and ask questions as to why she was so distraught. They would gossip, and she didn't want that. She knew they found the murder weapon. She thought her hiding place was foolproof, but Jenn had found it. Soon they would be questioning her. She was thinking of leaving the apartment in Chelsea. No one knew of her whereabouts or where she was living. After thinking it over, Ziggy settled on a plan: she would go underground until things calmed down. The investigation into his murder would reveal her secret. No one would wonder about her, as she remained like a ghost in the night after all.

CHAPTER 3

MINNIE MCCRACKEN WAS in at 7:00 a.m. and read the report that the nursing aide, Ziggy, did not report to work that morning. Minnie knew the position was difficult for some of the aides, but she was surprised when Ziggy did not show up. Ziggy worked on Mansard 6 with Father Pat.

"I'm very surprised she's not here," reported Father Pat.

"We've called her contact number, and it was a bogus number. The address she gave us was an old warehouse. None of the contact information was correct. I'll talk to some of the other aides and see if I can get some more information."

This was the least of Minnie's problem today. The state surveyors were investigating an alleged abuse case. One of the patients fell and was found with bruise marks all down her arm. This patient resided on the Alzheimer's unit. The family noticed the bruises and immediately called the police and the state. *It may have all been coincidental*, thought Minnie. A lot of the patients were thin and bruised easily just from repositioning.

Father Pat returned to his duties on Mansard 6. He was in the middle of the morning medication pass when he noticed one of Ziggy's friends.

"Hey, Alice, do you know where Ziggy is this morning?"

"I have no idea, Father. I don't know too much about Ziggy personally. She doesn't share much or talk about her life outside of here. The only time I've ever seen a reaction from her was when Father Don was murdered."

Father Pat thought about that last comment. Father Don did spend a lot of time with Ziggy when he was visiting. *I never thought about it before, but now that Alice mentioned it, they were together frequently*, he thought.

Minnie continued on her morning nursing rounds. She recently was questioned regarding her activities on the day of Father Don's murder. She wasn't crazy about Detective MacDonald and wished the whole brouhaha would disappear. Now that they found the murder weapon, she was sure they would have more clues as to who was the perpetrator. Minnie finished her ward rounds and proceeded to the elevator. She was stressed out, and it was beginning to show. She entered the service elevator and hit the button for the seventh floor, roof deck. No one had seen her get on the elevator. The elevator stopped on the seventh floor, but the door would not open. She hesitated before she pushed the alarm button. She tried the open button again, and this time it opened. She told the administrator she had a conference call that would keep her busy for the next two hours. Minnie pulled out an old chaise lounge that was hidden in the corner with some other chairs and old equipment that was not being used. *I better put this back in the storage shed after I finish*, she thought. Otherwise, the fire department would notice it on their yearly inspection, and she did not want to draw attention to that area. The day was sunny and there was a light breeze on the roof. Minnie opened the chair and settled herself in. From the roof she could see as far as L Street Beach. It was beautiful up there. She could smell a barbecue cooking in the backyard of a nearby house.

The houses were so close together that you could practically see into the neighbors' kitchens and see what they were cooking. The roof deck had some beautiful plants stored up there from patients who had died. Minnie would always water them and prune them when she was there. She could smell the sweet scent of a small potted rose bush that was left behind.

Minnie laid back in the chaise lounge. She opened the top of her blouse to get some of the day's sunlight. She was beginning to relax. She opened a small purse she carried that contained homemade rolled cigarettes. She giggled to herself. She lit the cigarette and the aroma of medicinal marijuana drifted off the rooftop. A mild breeze blew it off the rooftop location.

Minnie smoked two joints and began to relax. She fell asleep in the chaise until the sound of a beeper paged her. It was Father Michael. She looked at her watch and realized two hours had passed. She gathered up her things and sprayed some perfume on herself. She pulled the hand sanitizer from her purse and sprayed Binaca spray in her mouth. She pressed the elevator button, and she stepped in when it arrived. She pressed the button for the first floor. The elevator seemed to move in slow motion. It finally hit the first floor and the door opened slowly.

There stood Father Michael and Detective MacDonald.

Father Michael knew Minnie was on the roof deck. In the past year, Minnie was diagnosed with a mild form of Parkinson's disease. He noticed her tremors at times. The only way she could control it was with medicinal marijuana. He knew if Minnie had smoked that she was having a bad day and the tremors were beginning to get out of control.

He knew of her situation and kept it to himself. There was no need for anyone to know this. She did a thorough job as a nursing director, and medicinal marijuana had been approved for use in the state of Massachusetts. But approval for use did not mean she could buy it in Massachusetts, so she ordered it from an alternative healing clinic in Los Angeles. She knew a doctor friend who prescribed it for her tremors. There wasn't a second thought when she showed up to the dispensary. No questions asked.

Father Michael, Detective MacDonald, and Minnie proceeded to the conference room where it would allow for privacy. Detective MacDonald wanted information on the whereabouts of Ziggy Tena.

"I need to know everything about this lady, where she lives, her job in the home, and any information concerning her and Father Don. Her fingerprints were found all over the murder weapon. We know this as they match the computer system fingerprints that are in the electronic punch in system," said the detective.

"Minnie?" he asked.

"Well, all we know now is that the address she gave us was false as well as the phone number. I know she didn't drive a car. Sometimes she would take a cab to work. I do know she was here alone, and that her connection to Father Don occurred before beginning work here."

Father Michael squirmed in his seat.

"Father Michael, do you have anything to add?" the detective asked.

"I knew Ziggy before she came here. As a matter of fact, Father Don sponsored her to come to this country. She was a refugee in a camp on the outskirts of Kenya. Father Don was doing missionary work there and ran a clinic for the homeless and refugees. He went there yearly to minister to the poor, homeless, and sick. He met Ziggy and her brother and sister there. Father Don had been going to Kenya for over twenty years. He had sponsored many people who needed asylum in the United States or to come here for school. Ziggy didn't harm Father Don—she loved him. She probably got scared and was so saddened by his death that she could not stay here. Grief can make you do things you would not normally do." Father Michael paused.

"Father Don had his mission in Kenya. We went to seminary school together. He knew of my time when I worked in Doctors Without Borders and was interested in African missions."

"We will need to contact the missions in Kenya to further investigate her background," the detective stated.

"Good luck with that, Detective. There are no records or computers there to trace her. This is a third-world country that we are talking about. Also Ziggy might not even be her real name; she may have changed it when she entered the United States. She did stay here at the home for a while, as Father Don asked me to put her up in one of the empty rooms. She stayed for over a year and went to school through the Red Cross to become certified as an aide. She was very quiet and secretive, and I never felt the need to interrogate her," he said.

"That's about it, Detective. That's all we know," Minnie added.

"You'll contact me if you hear from her?"

"Absolutely, Detective, we will. If our meeting is finished, let me show you the way out. Detective, it is time for Mass, if you would like to attend the service. We have a visiting Jesuit with us today," Father added.

"Thanks again, Father, but I never mix my spiritual life with work."

He tipped his scally cap to Father Michael and headed on his way out the building and back to the station.

CHAPTER 4

Thirty Years Earlier

DONALD O'SULLIVAN GREW up on Adams Street in Dorchester, Massachusetts. He attended Saint John's Grammar and High School. His parents emigrated from Ireland and worked menial jobs to make ends meet. He was one of seven boys and worked after school at the local pharmacy delivering prescriptions. He loved to drive the beat-up car and race down the street as he was going through the neighborhood. His father told him many times to be careful driving, as he didn't have a license yet. Don did everything he could to have fun. He played pool late into the week-end nights and hung around with his friends as much as he could. While delivering prescriptions he sometimes experimented with the drugs and would get high from them, especially the narcotics.

He would sometimes steal the drugs for his friends and they would go sit on Wollaston Beach and swim at night in the summer. Donald knew this wasn't right, but he wanted to escape from the day-in and day-out responsibilities he had in helping out with the family. He soon left working in the pharmacy and started to work in construction with his father and his father's friends. He marveled at the process of constructing a home or a school with one's own hands. This was probably why Donald was good at the craft as well. He was training to become a carpenter when tragedy stuck. His father had a heart attack on the job. Donald was devastated, as were his mother and siblings. This sealed his fate, and now the responsibility was on his shoulders. He found the burden of supporting his family at a young age very overwhelming. He sought relief by popping pills and smoking pot on the street.

It wasn't easy to find pot on the street corner, so he would venture into down town Boston near Park Street, where he always had success. One night while he was buying some dope, the dealer offered him some LSD. He took it, not realizing it was so powerful, and sat in the Boston Common all night. During this LSD encounter, he was so frightened that he began to pray to God. Surprisingly God responded.

He felt an overwhelming sense of peace and happiness he had not felt before. God told him this was not his plan for his life and that it was time to make some changes. Even though he had all this responsibility, God was calling him to a different life. Donald slept on the Common that night. No one came by to wake him.

Suddenly the sun came up, and Don was near the duck pond, watching the mother duck with her chicks, swimming peacefully along the gentle stream of water. Don thought of his mother and siblings and knew they would be OK without him. He picked himself up and vowed never to take drugs again and promised to follow God where he would lead him. Don then went home and told his mother he was thinking of joining the seminary. His mother was so happy for him and assured him they would be fine. His mother had accepted a job at the telephone company just that morning, and it had quite a few benefits that would help the family out.

Don knew God saved his life during that encounter and anything could have happened to him, but God had other plans. He knew this calling was not the usual experience most people would have to be called to a religious life, but Don knew it was real. He entered seminary school in Washington, DC, in September of 1978, and there he met Father Michael. They became instant friends. Father Don was always interested in Father Michael's stories of travels in Africa, especially of his time in Ethiopia. He spent three years in seminary school, and when the opportunity arose to travel on a mission post, Don took it. He landed in Kenya. The weather was very hot. Fortunately there was no humidity.

The chapel for the priests was a small wooden structure. After a few weeks in Kenya, Father Don encouraged some of the local townspeople to help to rebuild the mission. Being a carpenter in his younger years,

Father Don knew what he had to do. From the little money he had, he went to a makeshift lumber yard in Kenya and bartered for wood, nails, and hammers. He literally sold what he had taken with him to Kenya: extra clothing, shoes, blankets, and chocolate. In no time, Father Don had demolished the wooden structure and started to rebuild the chapel with whatever resources he had.

Soon the local tribesmen of the area heard of his good deeds and decided to help him. Every morning when he awoke, he would see a small crowd gathering at the work site.

Many of these people had meager ways of feeding their families or themselves, so instead of monetary reimbursement, Father Don would offer them a meal. Father Don did live in a priest's residence that had a dining hall. Soon the dining hall became a soup kitchen, and whatever food he had, he shared with the others. Word began to spread about their work at the mission. In less than two months, the chapel was rebuilt with a small infirmary in the back. Father Michael was to visit, and Father Don had plans for him in the mission.

Considering his experience and medical background, surely he could help with the clinic.

With some assistance from Save the Children and the Red Cross and other organizations, help and supplies poured in for the medical clinic. Within a year's time, Father Michael was now traveling and staying with Father Don. Some of the local people in the village who had medical training donated their time. Other doctors came from Doctors Without Borders and trained some of the staff. A lot of the patients there were children and mothers, suffering from malnutrition. What food supplies they had, they shared. Food insecurity was rampant. Most of the staples were beans, lentils, rice, barley, and wheat.

Some organizations donated dry milk, but reconstituting it was a problem. Often the water supply was contaminated, so it had to be treated before drinking. Protein sources were limited, and sometimes Father Don and the other friars would take a day's journey into the village to buy lamb meat for the rectory.

Father Don traveled back and forth from Kenya for over twenty years. He set up a refugee camp for survivors of war-torn nations nearby. This is where he ultimately met Ziggy and her siblings. It took many years to get her out of Kenya and immigrate to the United States because of the bureaucratic policies in both countries. He had helped many others immigrate to the United States. When Father Don returned, he wanted to be close to his family and settled in Dorchester, becoming the pastor for St George's Parish. Father Michael left as well and took up his post as an administrator for the Mansard House. They both felt it was time to come home.

During his time in Africa, Father Don's mother passed away. By this time all the boys had grown and some moved away with their own families. He had many nieces and nephews, and they all made a point of getting together during the holidays, weddings, and even funerals.

Father Michael thought of those times in Africa as being some of the most precious times in his life. He didn't talk too much about his past, only when he could reminisce with Father Don. Now those days were gone and they only lived in his memory.

CHAPTER 5

VISITATION HOURS WERE over. Crystal Darcy drove down the I- 93 South Expressway to her home in Milton. The midmorning traffic was not too bad. The Darcy's' home was on the books as a historical home south of Boston. It had been restored to the exact replica of the original home from 1789. However, it was practically rebuilt inside. The beautiful chandeliers and butler's pantry as well as the ornate front door were all original to the house. All of the pine floors were refurbished and brought authenticity to the beautiful home. Her father loved this house. Crystal was not too happy with the furnishings or the decorating. She preferred a more modern and contemporary home. She had plans for the house in the future. Her brother, Tom, was not living at the house now. He left with his wife as they reconciled their marriage and now moved away to Plymouth.

Crystal was the caretaker. Her mother loved this house and had many gatherings here when she was growing up. She often thought of her mother. She was always so concerned about what everyone thought. She belonged to this women's group and that sodality. She was always fund-raising for some beautification project. Crystal found her mother's constant involvement in the community tiresome. Crystal worked for a living. Unfortunately, her mother squandered her father's money and never worked a day in her life.

Her father's money was currently being used to pay for his care at the Mansard.

No, there was no free ride for the Darcy's. Only at the time of her father's death would the inheritance be passed down to her brother and herself. Crystal supported herself by working as a paralegal in Boston. The pay was enough for one person to live on, but certainly not what she was accustomed to.

Her father had written in his will that no inheritance would be transferred to his children if they were not independent, on their own, and paying their own bills. Mr. Darcy himself worked all his life to support his family and acquired quite a fortune in the antique business. The house foyer displayed some of the original artwork of Degas and Picasso. They were worth a pretty penny, and Crystal had no intention of letting them out of her sight.

She moved into the kitchen area and put on the kettle for some tea. She opened the refrigerator to see if there was anything she could salvage for supper. For all her complaining, Crystal was actually quite the homemaker. She originally started school at the Culinary Institute in Boston and had accrued an advanced knowledge of cooking techniques. She was finishing up her last semester when her mom got sick with lung cancer. Surprisingly, her mother did not smoke. Crystal was not allowed to smoke in the house, so she would often have a cigarette or two outside in the flower garden patio. Her mother slept with the window open. Crystal often wondered if her mother was inhaling secondhand smoke, as Crystal smoked on the floor below, and the smoke wafted upward. Much like the cigarette smoke, this memory hung over her head.

The kitchen was modernized with a cabinet refrigerator, custom ceramic floor, and all stainless steel appliances. The open floor plan and large kitchen island was equipped with all the modern technology that any chef would envy. Crystal pulled out two chicken breasts from the freezer and thawed them in the microwave. She was preparing to dredge them in egg and flour when the phone rang.

"Hello, may I speak with Crystal Darcy, please?"

"This is she. Can I help you?"

"This is Detective David MacDonald, and I am investigating the murder of Father Donald O'Sullivan."

Crystal sighed and braced herself.

"I would like you to come to the station regarding the murder investigation."

"This sounds serious, Detective, should I be concerned?" she asked.

"Ms. Darcy, you can retain an attorney if you wish, but we still need to ask you a few questions regarding Father Don and your father's relationship," he stated.

"Can I come after work tomorrow?"

"I'll see you then, Ms. Darcy. Just ask for me at the front desk. Till then, good night."

Crystal suddenly lost her appetite and dumped her supper in the trash. She snatched a bottle of wine from the wine refrigerator and headed upstairs for the evening. Crystal thought, *Is he crazy, does he think I had anything to do with Father Don's death? That's absurd. Although with my brother's history of violence, I wouldn't put it past him.*

* * *

The next morning as Crystal was getting ready for work, she heard her brother's car pull up in the driveway. Tom Darcy was upset that Crystal was called down to the station to be interrogated. He wanted to know what Detective MacDonald said to Crystal.

"Not much. He wants me to answer a few questions," Crystal answered.

"Be careful what you say, Crystal. Our private life is none of his business," Tom whined.

"He's a trained investigator, Tom. If there is something he suspects, trust me, he'll get it out of you. What are you worried about? There's nothing to hide, is there? Unless you mean your little outburst you had with Father Don the day before he was murdered. What were you arguing about anyway?"

"Nothing, just forget about it. You didn't see or hear anything. Got it?" Tom said.

"Got it. Jeez, don't get yourself worked up. You need to control your temper, Tom. Your blood pressure is going to skyrocket. You're wound so tight."

"That's enough, Crystal," he said. "Case closed!"

Crystal finished her day up quickly. She left work around three o'clock to go down to the precinct. She asked for Detective MacDonald at the front desk. On her way in, she saw Father Michael leaving. She wondered what he told the detective about her and her family.

"Good afternoon, Crystal, please come in."

Crystal entered what looked like an interrogation room that had an obvious two-way mirror.

"Crystal, on the day of the murder, March fourth, where were you?"

"I was at home preparing to come and visit with my father."

"What was the relationship between you and Father Don?" the detective asked.

"Father Don visited my father because he was a parishioner at St George Church. My father enjoyed his company. My mother and he belonged to the church and were Eucharistic ministers at Mass," she said.

"What about you? Did you know Father Don?" he asked.

"Not really. The Mass on Sunday morning was usually an older crowd; Father Don would say that Mass. I would attend the four o'clock Mass on Saturday, if I went at all. I didn't run into him much," she said.

"Did you like Father Don?"

"I can't say that I cared for him either way. It was my father, basically, that was friendly with him."

"Crystal, is there any reason that you or your brother would want Father Don out of the picture?"

"That's a terrible thing to say, Detective."

"Isn't it true that Father Don was to inherit a sum of money, to be donated to the church, at your father's passing? Isn't it true, Crystal, that you were trying to have the will changed, so that no charities were to receive any funds, and that you threatened Father Don to stop interfering in your family, or else?"

"What are you implying, Detective? I refuse to answer another question till I speak with an attorney."

"That would be advisable, Crystal," he said cheekily.

"Am I free to go?"

"Well, I can't keep you, you're not a prisoner."

With that, Detective MacDonald showed Crystal to the exit and tipped his cap to bid her good day.

"You are always a gentleman, right, Detective?" Crystal offered sarcastically.

"Of course, Miss Crystal, I wouldn't behave any other way!"

She turned to him and glared.

"My attorney will be in touch."

* * *

Tom Darcy headed home to Plymouth. The drive was crowded, as it was rush hour.

He needed to get home to move some things into the basement, articles that he had removed from his father's estate before he moved out. Insurance, in case his inheritance didn't work out the way he planned it. Tom was going to make sure he had what was rightfully his, even if it wasn't left in the will. He was certain his mother would have wanted him to have these things. Tom pulled into the driveway of his ranch-style home, which was close to the beach in Plymouth. His wife, Claire, was already preparing his dinner in the kitchen. He entered through the attached garage and headed downstairs before greeting her.

In the basement he had an old cedar chest with a lock that he could store things in. He took out his keys and put the key into the padlock he had put onto the chest. With a strong pull, the chest opened, and Tom starting assessing the fortune he had amassed thus far. He had expertly replaced the paintings in the foyer with counterfeit paintings. Crystal hadn't a clue that Tom still had the spare keys to the house and had been secretly taking things while Crystal was at work. He already had his mother's jewelry collection replaced. The diamonds were replaced with cubic zirconia, and most of the gold was replaced with cheap knock-offs. Today Tom took the silver tea service that was his grandmother's and replaced it with a lookalike tea service. Crystal would never know.

CHAPTER 6

FATHER MICHAEL HURRIED back to the rectory after his daily walk around Pleasure Bay. He tried to figure out how his Swiss Army knife ended up not only in Mr. Darcy's room, but stabbed into the body of his dear friend. Father Michael knew it was stolen from him. He tried to think where he left it last, and the only place he could recall was where he usually left it, in his top right dresser drawer. That would mean that someone entered his room, went through his things, and deliberately took it. He tried to review in his mind the last person who might have been in the rectory.

Oftentimes, family members would meet in the living room downstairs to discuss finances and the care of their loved ones. Visiting clergy also frequented the rectory, and it was not uncommon for the rectory to have an out-of-town guest. He was very disturbed that Ziggy's fingerprints were all over the murder weapon. The match was confirmed by the new punch in system that required a fingerprint for identification. As he told the detective down at the precinct, he really doesn't recall when or how it went missing. Someone stole it, yes, but who?

As of today there was an all-points bulletin out for Ziggy, and her picture was plastered all over the TV. *She must be so frightened*, Father thought. The media could convict someone before there was ever a trial. He knew Ziggy would not be found, not with the African underground in America. He had seen people disappear, never to be found. Fortunately Father Michael was cleared as a suspect. He was relieved for that, but it would not bring his dear friend back.

The census in the home began to pick up after he was cleared as a suspect, and it was back to business as usual. Mr. Darcy continued to be guarded daily, and the family seemed to be visiting more than usual. Probably, he thought, more to watch their father decline rather than help him. Oh, the things you see families do when money is involved! It's not a Christian thought, he sighed to himself, but the truth isn't always pretty.

Minnie McCracken met Father Michael in the hall.

"It seems we have all been cleared as suspects," she began. "The investigation is focusing on Ziggy."

"I'm not sure if that is where it should be focused, but I'm sure the police know what they are doing," Father Michael said.

"I didn't let the detective know, but on the day of the murder, I did see Father Don talking a lot with Mr. Darcy. He seemed to stay in the room for a while. They weren't arguing, but Mr. Darcy seemed to be upset about something…but maybe it was nothing," she said.

"Well, we know that's not true. It's hard to tell with someone who has his type of dementia. Patients could get very paranoid and speculate as to all sorts of ideas in their heads that aren't always grounded in reality."

"Also Father, there were a few visiting friars in the chapel that morning that I have never seen before. Were you aware of them visiting?"

"I'm not sure, Minnie. I will have to check my calendar to see if they were invited guests or just visiting for the Mass. Sometimes the friars from Park Street Church come by to hear the Mass if they are visiting nearby."

Father Michael left Minnie in the hallway and proceeded to his office. He immediately went to his calendar to check on that day. There were no scheduled visits. He checked the books for the required signatures, but there weren't any from visiting priests.

How did these three friars get into the building without signing in and without my knowledge? There was only one person would be able to do that: Father Pat.

Father Pat was on duty on Mansard 6 the day the friars came to the front door. Security called him down to the front desk and allowed them to proceed to the chapel as they identified themselves as friends of Father Michael. In the case of any of the clergy, they were never asked for identification, as they were always welcome at any rectory that was Catholic.

Father Pat was not at all suspicious and believed that's what they were here for: Mass and a friendly visit. He didn't chat with them long as he was needed back on the floor. He failed to mention this to Father Michael at supper that evening as he actually forgot, with all the commotion in the home and the event of Father Don's death.

Father Michael could not believe this. What was happening here?

Father Michael thought of another possibility. There was a Friar residing in the building, Father Emmanuel. He was very sociable and enjoyed the company of the other friars. That was probably it. Father Michael made a note to himself to talk to Father Emmanuel about this. He also served in Ethiopia and stayed near Addis Ababa at a mission on the outskirts of the city. He once told him the people were so poor there but they were peaceful people and did the best with what they had. Father Michael agreed with him on that. Father Emmanuel was always available to listen to any of the staff or residents and would offer his wise words and counsel. He was well loved in the home, and Father Michael respected his practical ways and ability to get to the truth of the matter. He made a mental note to visit him later.

Meanwhile there was work to do. Father Michael had to get back to the business of running the home. He made his way back to his office to finish writing his budget reports to send to the main rectory. The accountant for the Mansard House was waiting for his final report. Father Michael had many plans to renovate the home.

First he wanted to bring in an outside vendor to set up a coffee shop for staff and patients to have a place to go for their lunch and when family visited. This would produce income for the home because he was planning to rent out the space with its own independent staff. This way he would not be responsible for running the shop but would be paid for the renting the space. Of course whoever did this would need to comply by all the state and federal regulations required in a nursing home.

Second he wanted to purchase some of the property nearby to start an assisted living house. Of course this property was near the beach, but he thought how wonderful this would be for the elderly inhabitants. As Father wrote up his report, the phone rang. It was a strange voice that sounded muffled.

"Father, there is still some work to be done. We expect you to get the charitable donations for the Darcy estate signed as agreed in the will. There is no debate in this. You will do this as agreed with Father Don or you will pay the consequences."

"Who is this?"

Father Michael was shocked. *Why are these people calling me and why are they threatening me?*

"Mr. Darcy's will has nothing to do with me, and I will not pressure any family into donations to any organization!"

For a moment, Father Michael heard a faint mumble of recognition in that voice. Why was that voice familiar? Even though it was disguised, it sounded familiar.

Oh, the pressure was getting to him. He put on his coat and opened the bottom drawer of his desk. He pulled out a package of cigarettes and stuffed them into the zippered pocket of his jacket. Father Michael left through the front door of the home and told the receptionist, "I'll be gone for a while. I'm taking a walk around Castle Island. You have my cell number. You can call if you need me."

"Father Michael, don't forget your umbrella. It looks like there is a storm brewing."

Father walked down the front steps and looked upward toward the clouds. Indeed, there was a storm brewing. There certainly was.

CHAPTER 7

JENN HURRIED THROUGH the last of her duties for the day. It was a busy week and she was anxious to get home to start the weekend. When she arrived at home, her eight-year-old Lhasa apso was waiting at the door expectantly as she entered.

"Hey, girl, are you ready for your walk?" The dog eagerly followed Jenn to the dining room as she put her sneakers on. Jenn grabbed her leash and left through the back door. Walking always helped Jenn to think. She was thinking about all the events that transpired these past few weeks and suddenly felt deflated. All the questions, interrogation, and worry surfaced, and Jenn began to cry. *What is wrong with me?* she thought. Jenn had a good cry, sighed, and took a big breath as she continued to walk. She watched the flowers as she walked and waited for Holly to do her business. Some of the gardens were just beautiful. She always enjoyed watching things grow.

The homicide department cleared most of the staff as suspects this week. Knowing Ziggy was not only a main suspect but was still missing was nerve-wracking for Jenn. *Where could she be and what is she trying to hide from? If she had nothing to do with the murder, as Father Michael seems to think, why doesn't she come forward and clear herself?* Jenn was turning the corner as she saw her son returning home from work.

"Ma, what's up?"

"Not much," Jenn replied. "I'm taking Holly for her walk. It's been a difficult few weeks at work. It's getting to me."

Jenn's son, Jed, comforted her. "Relax, Mom, don't worry about it too much. Why don't we order a pizza and see if there is a good movie on tonight?"

"That sounds like a good idea, Jed. Dad will be home soon, he can join us."

"We'll just chill, Mom."

Jed was living at home till he finished his degree from the College of Music in Boston. He was a talented musician and started late at the College.. He was playing in a band called Jed and Friends and got many gigs to play locally.

Jenn's oldest daughter was like another mother in the family. She always made herself available to Jenn, and they both enjoyed the theatre and would wait for the next production to come to town. The Boston Opera House was their favorite venue.

Jenn had two more sons and two more daughters. Both the girls were on their own and the two boys, twins, were living in Maine working in the fishing industry. They started out as fishermen in Gloucester and then moved up to Portland, Maine. With all the construction and tourism in Portland, there was a lot of business from the seafood restaurants.

Jenn and her husband, Henry, tried to spend time with the children as much as they could. Usually for a month in the summer, the family would spend time at their summer home in York, Maine, near Long Sands Beach and have cookouts and get-togethers with all the relatives. Jenn and Henry were both from large families and enjoyed spending time with their extended family at their summer place.

Working at the Mansard, she would save all her vacation time for these few special weeks off. Oh, the Mansard. Her mind jumped back to all of the paranoia and nervousness floating about the nursing home. She knew Father Michael was feeling the strain of the murder and the financial problems occurring at the home. She recalled spotting him at a distance as she did her routine walk out to the jetty near Castle Island. He was smoking a lot lately. She enjoyed walking over there as she remembered her own special time with her mother and the long walks and talks they would have when visiting with her. Jenn's father was from South Boston, so she felt a connection to the neighborhood.

Working at the Mansard afforded Jenn the luxury of being near the ocean and being close to her old neighborhood in Dorchester. Sometimes after work she would drive to the Cemetery to visit her parents and stand at their grave, thinking about their lives and how much they sacrificed for their children. When you are young, she thought, you never think how your life will turn out, and how much your parents did for you. It's only when you have your own children that you recognize life lessons that you received as a child.

Jenn finished feeding the dog and went to lie on the couch to take a rest after her day at work. The phone rang. It was Lilian. "Turn on the Channel 5 News."

On the evening news, a breaking story was developing.

The news anchor said, "The main suspect in the murder of Father Donald O'Sullivan, Ziggy Tena, was arrested after she was found crossing the Canadian border today. Canadian authorities arrested her on false passport papers and trying to cross the border without proper identification. The suspect at this time is being taken back to the United States."

The Canadian border patrol overhead camera caught a picture of her just as she was crossing the border from Vermont, showing Ziggy in the driver's seat of a car. The words "Wanted in a murder investigation" scrolled across the bottom of the screen. Ziggy was unrecognizable on the TV. The only identifying clue was her teeth. When she smiled she had a big gap between her two front teeth that gave away her identity.

"Oh my God, Lilian. Can you believe this?"

"I can," replied Lilian. "It's a never-ending story."

With that, Lilian said her good-bye and wished Jenn a good night's sleep.

The next morning Jenn awoke early to listen to the news. She had the day off and wanted to start her errands early. Her house was quieter during the day with the boys gone on their own. Now she understood the phrase "empty nest" and didn't mind it at all. Her job took most of her time, but the housework and laundry were taxing on her. Jenn was approaching sixty years old, and she was feeling it. It didn't matter that she looked younger; her body told her otherwise.

She headed out to the backyard before the sun got stronger, to finish up planting her sunflower seedlings. She had a vision of the backyard as a serenity garden, a place to read, rest, and have family gatherings. She had planted marigolds, lavender, cosmos, and had three beautiful rose bushes that she planted herself and watched them grow up, a lot like children. She planted tomato plants and peppers at the beginning of June, and they were growing fast. Wherever she could find room, she threw a pot of flowers or vegetable plants to fill up the yard. On her back porch the pots of morning glories started to hook onto the lattice fence, enclosing the porch. She could sit in the kitchen early in the morning and see the blooming flowers as she sipped her tea. She tried to make a happy and peaceful home for all of the family.

Soon it was noon, and the sun was beaming full force. Jenn decided to go in, have her lunch, and watch the midday news. She turned on the television in the kitchen to listen again as they announced the arrest of Ziggy Tena. But this report was not like the night before; this report revealed something different. When Ziggy was arrested, the child that was traveling with her, a little five-year-old boy, was taken into child services. Jenn was stunned. She had never once heard Ziggy talk about a child, let alone her own. She turned to click off the television as the soap opera *As the World Turns* started. Jenn repeated to herself, "As the world turns, indeed," as she shook her head in amazement.

CHAPTER 8

ZIGGY GAZED AT the stained and moldy ceiling of the holding cell in the precinct. She knew she was in trouble now with the authorities and was afraid she might be deported. *This cannot happen*, she thought. *I didn't spend all this time coming to America just to be sent back. Of course, I will tell the authorities what I know, and they will let me go. I'm in America, I have rights. Of course, we're in a civilized country with rules and procedures.* Ziggy was not afraid here. This was a country club. She thought back to her arrest in Ethiopia, after being accused of disagreeing with the government. She was thrown into a wooden jail with a dirt floor. She had known then that her survival depended on getting out of that place. Her parents were gone. She was in charge now and had to get her brother and sister into safety. They were brought to an orphanage.

Back in Ethiopia, Ziggy tricked the guard into her cell. She found an old steel cross under the mattress where she was sleeping and hit him on the head as he turned his back. He collapsed to floor, and she leaped over his body and ran as fast she could. Ziggy was an avid runner. It was her dream to come to America, and her ticket out was through running. She had trained with the elite runners and knew she would make it out. She ran through the streets and slowed down in the Mercado. It was late but still very crowded, and no one was watching her. She ran and ran all night till she was very far away from the city. She turned to look behind her, and still no one was following her. She knew that would be short-lived, though: they had cars and she had legs. As she slowed to a jog, she thought of her brother and sister who were still at the orphanage. She stopped to rest near a willow tree.

Her cousin NuNu lived nearby on a farm with her family. NuNu had no idea of Ziggy's dilemma. Ziggy would not tell her, either. Ziggy crafted a plan in her head quickly. At night she would travel to the orphanage and, when her siblings were ready, help them escape. Her uncle had an old horse and wagon that he used for selling eggs and wheat. She would steal that and leave it where he could find it. Ziggy knew she did not have much time.

After she rested, she walked to her cousin's farm. She told her cousin NuNu to go and visit the children and tell them she would be there that evening. NuNu packed clothes and food for them to last for a few days. She didn't ask Ziggy too many questions. She knew Ziggy had her reasons not to share her plans with her. NuNu did what her cousin asked. There were many farms along the way where the elders would welcome her to rest, and she would travel by night. Ziggy disguised herself with country clothing, farmer's clothes that they could wear while traveling. No one would be looking for a student among the farmers, so she felt at ease during dinner with her cousins that evening.

Ziggy did not tell them too much, just that she was passing through on her way to her friend's home in the next village. The less they knew, the better. Her cousin NuNu showed her how to get to a safe house that would lead her in the right direction. NuNu knew that she would be safe with this family and they would lead her to the next destination.

That evening she traveled with the horse and wagon. She blended in with all the other farm people. She snuck into the orphanage area and saw her brother and sister as they returned from their evening meal. They were with the missionaries' orphanage, and she was not going to leave them here. While standing there she heard something fall behind her. When she went to look, she saw a petite nun in brown garments with a cross around her waist.

"It's OK, dear, don't be nervous, I'm here to help you," she whispered. "I know of your plight. Come with me, I will give you some extra robes that you can disguise yourself with while traveling during the day. There are a lot of sisters here that travel with the children to other orphanages during the day, so it should be safe for you."

Ziggy did what she advised and jumped down from the cart. "I'm here for my brother and sister. They will be coming with me. That's all you need to know, Sister. Let me into the orphanage, and I will get them."

Sister took Ziggy to where her siblings were. She hugged them and told them to quickly gather their things and come with her. Sister bid Ziggy farewell and she left very quietly.

Meanwhile the prison guard was gathering up other guards to look for Ziggy.

They gave up soon thereafter as they passed through the Mercado and were interrupted by a robbery in progress. They needed to calm the crowd and ended up staying to arrest the robbers.

Soon, Ziggy Tena was far from their minds.

The next five days were endless hours of travel that lasted into the night. They rested by day and continued on, at night, while the country slept. They went from farm home to farm home, without stating their destination but only to rest awhile and replenish their supplies.

Every day she put on her nun's robes and walked with the children. No one stopped them. She said a prayer to herself daily and thanked God for putting that nun in her path. In five days she arrived at the border of Kenya and freely walked over the border.

It was a few days later that she was found with her siblings and welcomed into the shelter. Every person at the shelter was coming from somewhere. Ziggy kept to herself as she did not want to reveal too much about her past, in case there were spies who would report back to the authorities. Sometime after that, she heard of a Mission that would help refugees immigrate to the United States. Here at the mission she met Father Don. At first she was hesitant to tell him her story, but then when she knew she could trust him, she told him of her plight.

Father Don was very sympathetic to Ziggy and familiar with her circumstances. There were many young people like her that had survived the trek across Ethiopia into the Kenyan missions. His first concern was their health and integration into the refugee camp. Ziggy was given a private section to live in with her siblings. Food and shelter came from different charities. When she was ready, Father Don asked her to help out with the babies in the shelter who were abandoned or left orphans of war. She loved the babies. At first she was hesitant to care for them but soon realized that all they needed was love and comfort, just as she did. Day in and day out Ziggy cared for and fed the little babies in the shelter. She enjoyed rocking them to sleep and found comfort in their snuggling warmth.

Soon she was managing the orphanage, organizing the older children, and helping with some of the teaching. Ziggy, after all, was a college student and was majoring in management and finance. She knew how to organize a budget, barter, and get the best price for goods. Soon everyone in the shelter, including Father Don, depended on her ability to organize people and her practical financial skills.

Father Don knew she wanted to go to America, but sponsorship was hard to come by for Ziggy and her siblings. Finally, he had an idea. There was a program where new mothers were allowed to immigrate to Israel. There were many priests there who oversaw the relics and sacred places of the Holy Land. He knew they would be able to sponsor her for temporary asylum, and then from there she could go to America. Despite Ziggy not being a mother, she and Father Don thought of a way to get her there: Ziggy would travel with one of the orphan babies and take him with her to freedom in America.

Considering Father Don's plan, she carefully thought about who she would take with her. There was one little baby that was well enough to travel and needed someone to take care of him. She took this baby as her own, and made it safely to the Missions in Israel. There she stayed with the baby and without her siblings. She would have to wait for now. She knew they were well and that Father Don was looking out for them. She planned on sending for them as soon as she was settled in America.

* * *

Ziggy woke with a start as she heard someone entering the cell. Detective MacDonald entered and sat down.

"Hello, Ziggy, we have finally found you. What do you have to say about all this?"

Ziggy smiled warmly.

"I know, Detective, once you hear my story you will remove me from your suspect list as you will realize I wouldn't hurt Father Don because I loved him."

"That's the story we want to hear. Although there is one problem: your fingerprints were all over the murder weapon. Can you explain that?"

"I took it because I knew it was Father Michael's, and I did not want him implicated in Father Don's death. He helped me so much when I first came here to this country, and I felt that I owed him something. I don't know who murdered Father Don, but I know for a fact Father Michael was not involved."

"And why should we believe that you were not involved?" he asked.

"Well, if you look at the schedule, I wasn't on duty that day and just happened to be in the building to pick up my paycheck. I was going to meet Father Don in the café, but when he didn't show up, I went back to the floor to see if I could find him. I came upon the all the noise and yelling and screaming. I saw Father Don on the floor as the nurses were trying to resuscitate him. I went into the room for just a moment and saw the knife under the commode and took it. I know now it was probably the wrong thing to do, but at the time I was in shock and it made sense to me. I'm sorry, Detective, that I've caused this problem for you," she said.

"Well, for now we will have to hold you here. You may want to get an attorney at this time so you have a way to get yourself out of this mess."

With that said, the door opened up and Attorney John McDevitt entered.

"Detective, I represent the Mansard Corporation, and I have been asked to represent Ms. Ziggy Tena, so if you have no warrant to hold her, I want her released into my custody."

"There was a warrant issued, so bail will be set. If she can't pay, maybe the judge will allow her to be on home confinement till they go to trial."

"If you have any further questions for her, you can contact me at this number." John McDevitt handed him his business card. "I'll see in you in court, Detective."

He proceeded to the chair and sat down. "I would like to talk to my client in private, Detective."

Detective MacDonald turned toward the door and left without saying another word.

CHAPTER 9

JOHN MCDEVITT RETURNED to the Mansard House to meet with Father Michael.

"Ziggy needs a trial lawyer," he explained. "I can only go so far with this. My specialty is corporate law. Of course, on behalf of the corporation, I can advise her, but we need a defense attorney, Father."

Father Michael knew this was true. If Ziggy were to get off free, she would need a good defense. Father Michael had some friends that were attorneys; he would see what he could do.

In the meantime, there were a few concerns he had. He needed to talk to Detective MacDonald about the situation with the three friars entering the home, unbeknownst to him. These friars had every opportunity to enter the rectory and could have stolen his Swiss Army knife. While chatting with Father Emmanuel, he mentioned the visiting friars, but Father Emmanuel stated he did not have any visitors that day. Father Michael checked all of his belongings to see if there was anything else missing. There were some beads and crucifixes missing as well as three brown cloaks. He would call Detective MacDonald in the morning, as this could be significant. Better yet, it might clear Ziggy as being a main suspect.

Father Michael needed to get out for a few hours. He left the building and started up his Volkswagen. Heading out left on West Broadway, he drove toward I-93 north. He needed to get away from everything. He drove up 93 and headed toward Route 1. On Route 1 he drove north till he reached Gloucester. He found the small Irish bar he frequented.

Father, wearing his street clothes, walked into the pub. He sat down at the old-fashioned bar. The bartender approached and put out his hand.

"What will it be today, Mike?"

"I'll have a gin and tonic on ice. Actually make it a double," he said.

"Right away!"

Father Michael then pulled out a pack of Pall Malls from his jacket and lit up his cigarette.

"Here you go, gin and tonic. Would you like something from the kitchen? It's still open."

"I'll have some fish and chips. Thanks, Joe."

"No problem, it will ready in a few minutes."

Father Michael sat at the bar quietly. He took a sip of his gin and tonic and then in one gulp swallowed it. *That should dull some of the pain*, he thought. Father Michael had excruciating back pain at times from an old compression fracture. He knew it was time to go back to the chiropractor, but he found his way of handling it was easier. He looked around the old bar. There were a few other men drowning their problems with a drink.

What he enjoyed most about the bar was its everydayness and the anonymity. Here, no one really knew he was a priest. To them he was just another customer. Running away was a good way to describe it. Being at this bar brought memories of Father Don. They would meet up here where no one knew who they were, and they could relax. He looked at the time and wondered where it went. Already two hours had passed. He paid his tab and waved good-bye to the bartender.

"See you next week, then." Joe waved.

Father replied, "Possibly." With that he walked out of the bar into the late afternoon sun.

Back at the Mansard, Father Pat was paging Father Michael and was a little concerned he could not find him. Today Father Michael was saying the memorial Mass at St George's for Father Don, and it was getting late. Father Michael heard the page as he walked into the rectory.

"I'm here, Father Pat, don't worry. I'm just running a few minutes late. I'll be down soon."

Father Michael went to his closet to get his Mass vestments. When he opened his closet, he had a feeling that someone had just been there rummaging through it. His clothes were in disarray, and items were moved around. Also his drawers were slightly ajar, which were not like that when he left. He thought maybe he should lock up his room when he left, but he really did not want to do that.

It had been a month since Father Don's passing. There was a good turnout in the church.

He saw Ziggy in the front row with her house arrest monitor around her ankle since the court allowed her to attend the Mass. Afterward they proceeded to the Cemetery where he was buried. Some of the friars and attendees stayed at the grave as Father said a small prayer about Saint Francis, as this was his order's patron saint. Father Michael saw three friars staring at him that he had not seen before.

"Good afternoon, Father." One of the friars stepped forward.

"I'm Father Tom. We are so sorry about Father Don's passing. We understand you were close friends."

"Yes," Father Michael responded, "like brothers." He paused with suspicion. "And your acquaintance to Father Don?" he asked.

"Oh, we served together in a parish in Rhode Island, in Pawtucket, for a short time. It was a very poor neighborhood. We all enjoyed his stay there."

"Well, it was nice to see you, and we're happy you attended the service. We're having a small reception at the Fireman's Hall in Dorchester. They will be serving a modest dinner and refreshments. You are welcome to attend."

"Thank you, Father, but we need to return home. You know how the traffic can be brutal on a Saturday evening," he replied.

"Oh yes. Well, thanks again for coming." He waved good-bye.

As he was getting in his car, he saw, out of the corner of his eye, Father Pat conversing with the three friars with an air of familiarity. Father Michael drove out of the graveyard, took a right turn, and proceeded down Morrissey Boulevard. *Hmm*, he thought, *the three friars*. He felt uneasy. *What's going on here, what is Father Pat up to?* he wondered. *This all looks highly suspicious.* He would contact Detective MacDonald tonight.

CHAPTER 10

BACK AT THE Mansard House, Lilian was busy attending to residents. There had been an outbreak of norovirus. Some of the floors were quarantined, and all the dining rooms were closed for the time being. There were signs everywhere about the symptoms and how to maintain proper hand hygiene to protect yourself and others.

Lilian was currently visiting with Mr. Darcy, as he had contracted the virus and was now hooked up to an intravenous solution of dextrose and normal saline. He was very dehydrated and his health had declined considerably since her last visit. The police guard was lifted the second week of the murder investigation, and Mr. Darcy was no longer confined to his room. Fortunately, this norovirus was contained to the Boston area and was only a twenty-four-hour bug.

Mr. Darcy was recently enrolled in hospice care. The family was concerned because Mr. Darcy was now completely confused, and the previous will that was written was still in place.

The question was now that Father Don had passed away, was that section of the will admissible in a court of law? Lilian was finishing up with her examination of Mr. Darcy when Crystal Darcy entered the room.

"Lilian, I would like to discuss my father's care. It seems to me that you people are trying to kill him. My God, look at how doped up he is. And this hospice care—isn't that end-of-life care?"

"Crystal," Lilian started, "we've been through this. Your brother is the health-care proxy, and he approved of hospice care. Frankly, if your father didn't have these safeguards in place, he would not be able to get the regularly scheduled pain meds that he needs. He has his own private aide that takes care of him daily. If you would like to speak with a social worker on the hospice team, I can arrange that for you. Otherwise, your father is very comfortable. As you know, he is now do not resuscitate, do not intubate, and no transfers to the hospital."

Crystal deliberately walked over to Lilian and slapped her across her face. Lilian fell backward a bit but steadied her feet so she would not fall.

Lilian grabbed a nurse in the hallway.

"Call the police and security, stat. I've just been assaulted by a resident's family member. Step away from me, Crystal," Lilian warned.

In five minutes security was escorting Crystal Darcy to the front waiting room to meet with the police. Father Michael rushed to the waiting room with the police and gave Crystal a stern warning and threatened to press charges. She was not allowed to enter the home till further notice.

Crystal started crying hysterically.

"But they are trying to kill my father. Don't you get it? My brother wants my father dead and this hospice thing is helping to do that."

Father Michael tried to calm her down, but to no avail. He asked the police to escort her home.

Father Michael was a little concerned about her mental health. She seemed somewhat paranoid. Sometimes family members would have behavioral issues when a loved one was nearing death. Yet he never saw someone react this outrageously.

Father Michael returned to the unit. On approaching he saw Lilian with an ice pack to her face.

"Let me look at that, Lilian. It doesn't look too bad, but she must have got you with her ring, because you are bleeding. Let me drive you over to the Saint's Hospital Emergency Room. You want that taken care of. You may need stitches."

"All right, Father. I'm going home after that. I'm done for the day. My husband will be furious when he sees me. I'm sure he will want to press charges, and so do I. I've had enough with that family," she said.

Lilian and Father Michael pulled into the parking lot of the Saint's ER and locked the car and proceeded to the entrance. While they were entering, they saw Crystal Darcy being escorted to the locked psych unit. Apparently Father Michael's suspicion was right. Crystal was suffering from an acute manic episode, probably brought on by her father's condition. Lilian turned away and guided Father Michael to the other side of the hallway.

"I knew there was something off with her today. That's good she's here, she can get the help she needs. It looks like they are transferring her to the psych unit. Come in this room, Father. I don't want her to see us."

The physician assistant on duty that day then entered the room.

"Good afternoon," she said, "my name is Donna Sullivan. What can I help you with today?"

Lilian looked at Donna, and Donna grinned. They both hugged each other instantly.

"Lilian, are you all right? Look at that cut! Let me take a look at that."

Father looked at Lilian in surprise. Lilian explained, "Father, this is Donna, my roommate from school. We went to Northeastern University together. We haven't seen each other in a few years."

"This looks like a deep cut. I'm going to clean it up and give you a few stitches. Hopefully it won't leave a scar. So, what, are you getting into fights these days, Lilian?" Donna teased.

"No, it's a long story, girl, for another time," she said, laughing. "OK then, I'll get you two signed out. You take care of yourself."

Donna left and looked at Lilian with her hand raised to her ear and mouthed the words, "Call me soon." She waved and went on to her next patient.

"How funny was that, running into my old roommate in the ER. What a day!"

Father Michael drove Lilian back to work. She went back to her office and got her things.

She left the building and went to get her car. As she approached her SUV, she saw a ticket on the window for twenty-five dollars. She shook her head and threw the ticket on the seat beside her. She then backed out of her space and drove up the hill and down around the beach. She headed north on the expressway toward Cambridge. Lilian arrived home forty-five minutes later. She had called her husband on the way to give him an update on the day's events. Needless to say her husband, James, was very upset. He saw her approaching and waited in the driveway till she got out of the car.

"How are you doing?" he asked in a worried voice.

"I'm OK, just a scratch and a few stitches. I'll survive," she said.

"Well, maybe we should press charges. This is very serious. I'll call the police tomorrow and we'll get the process started."

James was an attorney for a nonprofit organization in Cambridge that worked with human rights violations and was used to pressing charges. In fact, he felt that if you ignored violence against women, it might continue. Lilian knew why he reacted that way and just wanted to get a good night's sleep and forget about it for now. She entered the front hall and heard her kids in the kitchen arguing about something, probably supper. Lilian had six children, all girls, ages ten to twenty-six. She had her hands full. Her oldest daughter, Hillary, was at the counter starting to prepare a large salad. Hillary was graduating from Princeton with a law degree and was in the process of applying for a job, specifically one at her father's office. Lilian and Hillary were like two peas in a pod and very close. Lilian was very happy with Hillary's success. Lilian was happy to have her home, temporarily that is, while she was looking for her own apartment. Two of the older girls were away at college. The younger girls were fourteen, twelve, and the youngest was ten.

Lilian was considering working as a consultant soon as the demands of working full-time and having a large family were wearing on her. Her husband encouraged her to set up her own practice where she could basically make her own hours. When she saw her friend Donna, it brought back memories of when they were students and all the high hopes they had. These days there were so many different opportunities for physician assistants outside of long-term care. She would definitely call Donna tomorrow to catch up and ask if she knew of any job opportunities. She kept her thoughts to herself regarding changing her employment, but today's latest episode fed fuel to the flame. With that thought, Lilian changed into a tank top, shorts, and flip flops and helped Hillary prepare supper in the kitchen, as her youngest, Isabelle, hugged her around the waist.

The next day Father Michael called Detective MacDonald regarding the events that had occurred up to now regarding the three friars and the missing cloaks from the rectory. Detective MacDonald would investigate, but his first thought was that it was an innocent coincidence. He would talk with Father Pat to see what, if any, kind of relationship these friars had to Father

Don. The detective also planned to question Father Pat. It still remained unclear who was calling Father Michael about the inheritance money that would be left to the church. Detective MacDonald had other suspects in mind that might have wanted Father Don dead. Tom Darcy came to mind.

The news of Crystal Darcy's hospitalization in the psych ward spread through the house. Father Michael felt sorry for her and believed she did care for her father despite what people said about her. Tom Darcy, on the other hand, was waiting for his father to die, and for his inheritance. Already he was gathering his father's belongings and continued to do so while Crystal was hospitalized. He knew this time around she would be in for seven to ten days. She was transferred to the Psychiatric Hospital on her third day at Saints hospital. The psychiatrist felt Crystal might have been skipping her medications and suspected that the stress of her father's condition may have sent her over the edge. He prescribed Klonopin for her if her anxiety spiraled. Crystal was still talking about her brother's scheme to have her father admitted to hospice care. That was not the case, and Mr. Darcy was declining every day. He had now stopped swallowing his food, and the speech therapist downgraded his diet to puree. He was being fed all meals. He was only given what he would accept and was not forced to eat. It would only be a matter of time before the inevitable occurred.

The friars at the home had a vigil for every patient that was nearing death. This was very comforting to most families, except the Darcy's. Tom was still trying to appeal to his father to change the will, as he felt he was entitled to most of his wealth. The past few years, Crystal was the one who took care of him, before it became too much for her and he needed long-term care. She actually felt that the Mansard House did take good care of him up until this latest development.

The following Monday, Lilian returned back to work. Mr. Darcy's condition had declined considerably. She called the hospice nurse to adjust his morphine so he would not suffer during this transitional time. Later that day Mr. Darcy expired, just before the evening shift started.

Tom Darcy was called and came to stay with his father before he was taken to the morgue. Friends and relatives were called and informed of the sad news. Father Pat was at his bedside and performed the last rites. Just before Mr. Darcy expired, he called out for his daughter, Crystal.

Lilian was sad for the family and the suffering that Mr. Darcy endured, but felt he had a peaceful and painless passing. She gave her condolences to the family and proceeded to her office to write up the pronouncement. The attending physician was called and informed. Lilian called the Psychiatric Hospital and talked to the psychiatrist. He felt at this time that Crystal was too unstable to handle the news of her father's passing and asked Lilian to give her a few days. Lilian agreed but knew Tom might tell her anyway despite the doctor's advice. That's just what he did.

CHAPTER 11

FATHER PAT RETURNED to the rectory after his shift and headed toward his room. He closed the door and made a phone call. The recipient of the call was informed of the passing of Mr. Darcy and that the will, to his knowledge, was never changed and a considerable amount of money was to be left to the church. There was further conversation, and then Father Pat hung up the receiver.

Father Michael saw Father Pat return, and he picked up the receiver when he made his call. Father Michael was suspicious of Father Pat's activity and wondered why he was so concerned about what was left to the church. If there was a large sum of money donated, he would never see it. Mansard House did have some endowments from charitable organizations and some wealthy families.

Father Michael, after hearing the muffled voice over the receiver, recognized the caller. He thought it was Father Pat that had called him. What had he got himself into? Then he recalled Father Pat's past: before entering into the religious life, Father Pat did have a gambling problem. He once confessed during confession that he had a relapse and had lost quite a bit of money. Father Michael was afraid of that. It sounded like these so-called friars were pressuring Father Pat for his gambling debt. He would keep this information to himself for now and see where this would lead Father Pat. He did not want him to know that he was aware of the situation.

The funeral for Mr. Darcy was held in the chapel. There was a big crowd, and Crystal Darcy was so distraught she could not view the open casket. Her brother and his wife sat in the front row as the chaplain for the chapel said the funeral mass. Mr. Darcy was laid to rest at the neighborhood Cemetery in Milton.. His gravesite was located at the crest of a hilly slope near the cemetery florist. The ceremony at the grave was short. In her unstable state, Crystal tried to jump into the plot, but the pallbearers pulled her aside.

"Crystal, it's OK now, let Dad rest in peace. He suffered enough." Tom tried to console her.

"I don't ever want to speak to you again. You got what you wanted, didn't you? Tell your fat wife I never want to see her again, either!" she cried.

Tom looked at her and shook his head.

"There's no need to be insulting, Crystal."

Crystal left with Mr. Darcy's sister, her aunt Jane.

"Don't you worry now, dear. You come with me back to the house," she said.

Crystal turned toward her and put her head on her shoulder. She looked back at Tom accusingly.

Back at the house there was some mention of the will and when it would be read. Tom was the executor of his father's estate and planned to have the will read as soon as possible.

His father had a large estate and many investments and owned a formidable art gallery. Tom planned on contesting the will if in fact there was money left to Father Don. Crystal's share would not be considerable, he thought to himself.

Back at the Mansard House, Detective MacDonald was questioning Father Pat regarding his whereabouts on the day Father Don was murdered.

"I was on Mansard 6 passing out meds. I came running to the scene after a code two was called, just like everyone else," he said.

"I hear you let in some visitors that morning. Care to tell me their identities? Have you got something to hide, Father? Because if you do, I will get a subpoena and make you testify under oath about your involvement in this. Don't test me Father Pat. I'm known to have a temper."

"Of course I had nothing to do with Father Don's murder. You can't suspect me. We were good friends."

"The funny thing is, Father, your voice was recorded threatening Father Don regarding a personal matter. Were you in fact blackmailing him? Isn't that the reason you brought in the extra friars that morning? To scare him and remind him of the money that was promised to you?" Detective MacDonald said.

"You see, Detective, I will admit I had a bit of a gambling problem when I was in the Rhode Island parish. You have to understand I had a relapse and needed to come up with some money fast...I have some private information on Father Don that...well, yes, I guess you could say I was pressuring him. He was the treasurer of the friars' retirement fund. He handled all the investments, and I was just asking for a loan to pay back these people. They threatened my life."

"Did you steal the robes from the rectory for these three men, Father Pat?" Detective MacDonald asked.

"Well, I borrowed them, just for a short time. They didn't harm Father Don. They just went to have a friendly talk with him," replied Father Pat.

"Yes, I see, a friendly talk and then slit his throat. Then you secretly ushered them out through the back entrance, didn't you, Father? Don't deny it, we have you on the security cameras just as you opened the door to let them out. It's all on tape."

"That doesn't mean I killed him! I'm just as upset as everyone else around here about his passing. Please don't accuse me of things when you don't really know for sure what happened."

"Time will tell, Father. In the meantime I want the identity of those men, so I can take them in for questioning."

"I don't know their names. They worked for a Casino in Rhode Island. Obviously, I owed them money and they wanted to collect. If Father Don was in Mr. Darcy's will, I figured I could borrow a couple of thousand before it was put on record. What's the harm in that? Who would know?" he explained.

"Father, where's your conscience? Don't you know the difference between right and wrong?" Father Pat looked at him sadly and walked away without another word.

CHAPTER 12

MINNIE WAS HAVING a very bad day. She had just returned from her vacation in Nova Scotia. She was away for two weeks. She and her friend took a trip to Halifax up through Cape Breton and back to Yarmouth. They came back by ferry with their car on board. The scenery in Nova Scotia was breathtaking. Minnie enjoyed her time away from the Mansard. Now it was back to business as usual.

Her day was full of meetings. Lilian brought her up to speed on the latest scandal involving Father Pat and his gambling debt. Lilian knew about this because she overheard Father Michael on the phone explaining the circumstances to his superior. Father Pat was taking a sabbatical for one year at the monastery in upstate New York. They hired a new nurse to cover his duties on Mansard 6. Father Pat was very upset he had to leave his patients.

Minnie was glad to see him go. In reality she never really cared for him. He wasn't very supportive of the nurses and always had an attitude. For a priest, he wasn't very priestly. The treatment center in New York was where he needed to be. Minnie kept her opinion to herself; she did not want to upset Father Michael any further.

Lilian always liked Father Pat and felt sorry that he got himself into a bad situation.

As it turned out, the three friars were threatening his life and Father Michael paid off his debt from the retirement fund. In Father Don's absence, Father Michael was the treasurer of the retirement fund. Father Pat said he would find a way to return the money. Father Michael said it would be OK to pay slowly and not to do anything illegal to get it. He was in enough hot water as it was.

Minnie felt her tremors starting and realized she had missed a dose of her Sinemet. She went into her office and took her usual dose. She stayed in the office for long periods of time, as she did not want anyone to see her tremors. Lilian noticed right away that her condition had gotten worse. Some days the shaking was so bad that she could not go to work.

"Minnie, have you seen the neurologist lately? It looks like you may need an adjustment in your medication dose," Lilian said.

"Thanks, Lilian, but I think it's because I cut down on the dose. I don't feel good when I take it and thought I would try something else, a more alternative therapy. I've been using some marijuana that I got from a dispensary in Los Angeles. I don't use much, but it reduces my stress and the tremors. The dispensary recommended I try this strain of sativa ninety percent and indicia ten percent. Its street name is Brainstorm Haze. Also I'm going to acupuncture once a week. I'm also taking Coenzyme Q. All of it together seems to be keeping it at bay," she said.

"That's good, Minnie. Just stay on your meds and discuss it with the neurologist, please."

"I will, Lilian. Don't worry about me," Minnie replied. "Back to the issue at hand: What is your decision regarding Crystal Darcy? Have you decided to press charges?"

"No, I thought about it. With her father's passing, I don't think I will be seeing her anymore. I'll just let it go. What good is it going to do? It will probably add to her psychological problems. She obviously has enough to deal with. Crazy people go with the territory, right?"

"That's right, Lilian. People can get really crazy when they are under tremendous stress. It's our jobs as professionals to recognize that and not take it personally. Good decision, Lilian."

"Thank you, Minnie." Lilian left Minnie's office and continued with her busy schedule of patient visits and writing up her notes.

Minnie stayed in her office. She had other issues to deal with. She needed to discuss with the night nurses some reports of nurses sleeping on the job. The 11:00 p.m. to 7:00 a.m. shift was difficult, and Minnie was aware of that. The problem was some of the residents had very severe insomnia and could get into trouble if they started to roam around the facility while the nurses were sleeping. She tried to think of solutions before accusing anyone. This information was given to her through the suggestion box in the nurses' lounge area. Minnie would prefer that the person had come to her directly, but unfortunately that didn't always happen. She understood that. Needless to say if this was happening, it could also be reported to the state and jeopardize patient safety. Father Michael had suggested setting up a security camera on that unit, and then maybe they could see if this was really a problem.

What they found out was there was a security camera on the floor already that had been recording all along. Unbeknownst to everyone was that when they updated the security system to a digital system, they did not remove the old, outdated tape system. That evening the nighttime janitor found where the security tape was in the unused security office. All the tapes were still in place, as that office had been moved, and all the tapes were left. Fortunately the tapes were dated and went back a few months. Minnie knew it was going to be a long night and decided to start at the beginning.

One of the tapes showed that, one night around 2:00 a.m., one of the residents was walking around the floors and going into other residents' rooms. It seemed like he was taking things with him but was unaware of it. This wandering lasted around an hour, and then the resident returned to his room.

Minnie didn't recognize the resident, but she would check with Lilian before the day was out. The good thing was that she did not see anyone fall asleep on the job, so she wondered who'd written the complaint. The possibility that it was a disgruntled employee did pass Minnie's mind. In the meantime she needed to get back to work. New student nurses from Mass General Hospital would be starting today for their long-term care rotation, and Minnie needed to meet with them.

As she was walking down toward the auditorium, she ran into Father Michael.

"Hello, Father Michael, how's everything with you today?"

"Not well, Minnie. This whole situation with Father Pat has the other friars very upset. Also, the Friar Council may not even let him back here to work as a nurse again."

"Well," Minnie replied, "maybe it is for the best. He did jeopardize patient safety allowing those people into the building, not to mention the staff's safety. In today's world we need to be very careful."

"I understand your feelings, Minnie, but remember Father Pat is my friend and a brother in the faith, and I don't think he would do anything to hurt anyone intentionally. He just got mixed up with the wrong people, and it triggered a problem that was latent. *Thank God none of the residents were hurt.* He thought. As you know Minnie I am increasing the security staff. I don't want anything like this ever to happen again!"

"I'm sorry, Father. I didn't mean to imply anything untoward," she said.

"Enough said. Let's get back to work. Have a good, productive day now." Father Michael then turned the corner and proceeded onward to the rectory.

The rectory was an attached building that was connected by a hallway and then a door that led to the priest's quarters. The rooms were decorated simply and sparingly, and there was a bare dining room for their meals. Another hallway led to a beautiful living room with dated but very comfortable furniture. Father Michael had the largest bedroom, which also doubled as an office space for him.

He went into the bathroom cabinet and took two aspirin and a cool washcloth. He headed to his room to lie down for a short rest. A knock on the door interrupted his rest.

"Oh, hello Father. I'm sorry to disturb you. I thought you might like a nice cup of tea and some Irish bread. I just baked it this morning."

"That would be lovely, Christina," Father replied.

Christina was the friars' housemaid and cook. She was from Brazil, but she learned to make all of Father Michael's favorite foods. She was very fond of him and very happy to serve them.

She kept their home very tidy and clean. She also was an excellent cook and rotated their meals to include everyone's favorite meal once a week. She also introduced them to foods from her own country, which they enjoyed. There were ten friars that lived in the rectory. Most of the friars served as missionaries in other countries before they came here. Not everyone worked at the Mansard House. Some of the friars worked at the Pine Street Inn in Boston, serving meals in the soup kitchen and counseling the homeless. Others volunteered at a Rehabilitation Hospital in Jamaica Plain as pastoral counselors for the mentally ill and drug addicts. Another friar, Father Bob, was a journalist and ran the publication, *A Friar's Life: Walking with Saint Francis*. In the rectory was a beautiful meditation room for the fathers, with ornate stained-glass windows depicting the Stations of the Cross.

In Father Michael's room, there were pictures of his parents and brothers and sisters when they were young, back in Killorglin, Ireland. His parents had a hard life. Father Michael was the oldest of thirteen children. He suddenly thought of his mom's home cooking. She was a busy woman. She worked as a cleaning lady in order to put food on the table. She was a meticulous housekeeper as well. The house was always tidy and everyone had their chores to do daily. She kept everyone in line. If you didn't do your chores, you'd get a smack on the back of the head. No one messed with Mom. She was stern but loving. She reveled in her children's success, no matter how small. Father Michael knew what it was like to be poor. His dad worked just as hard as a bricklayer.

The dinner meal was the best time of the day for the family. If you got to the table late, there might not be supper left. Oftentimes he had bread and butter for supper. His parents passed away years ago, and most of the family was in the States. A few brothers stayed behind and still lived in the house his father built. His plan was to retire there when the time came. A knock on the door interrupted his thoughts.

"Here is your tea, Father, enjoy. Are you not feeling well?" she asked.

"Oh, I just had a little headache and needed a rest. The tea and bread will help with that. Thank you, Christina."

She closed the door quietly to allow him to rest.

* * *

Minnie had finished with her orientation and was back in her office with Lilian to review the tapes. It was hard to tell just who the resident was that was wandering, as the tape recording showed him only from the back.

"I really don't know who that is, Minnie," Lilian said.

"Well, there are thirty tapes, so I'll go through them all and see what comes up. My main concern is to see if any nurses were sleeping on the night shift. The tape I did see was fine, except for the wandering resident. This occurred after the nurse did her rounds."

Suddenly the alarm went off for a fire drill. Minnie and Lilian left the tape for the time being and hurried to the auditorium until the drill was all clear. She left the tape running in the VCR. The wandering resident was back on the screen, but this time he was facing the camera.

CHAPTER 13

ZIGGY WAS STILL confined to her room. Social services returned her son to her. This made Ziggy very happy and relieved. Everything was OK as long as her little boy was safe. Her mind kept wandering off to Father Don's face. When she looked at her boy, she was reminded of all Father Don had done for her and how much she missed him. People would be upset if they knew he was sponsoring her family to come to this country. The only one that knew of her situation was Father Michael, Sami's godfather. In fact Ziggy and Father Don were planning to get married. He loved Ziggy with all his heart.

He was planning on leaving the priesthood as now he had a child. Sami was, in fact, Father Don's child. He was very light skinned, but he had Ethiopian features. No one could really tell that he was mixed. Father Don was much older than Ziggy. She saw nothing wrong with this since most of the men from her country were married to much younger women. She did feel bad he was going to leave the priesthood, but he said it was time for him. He was still going to continue in the Order but as a layperson.

It happened all so suddenly between them. Their love was so strong that nothing could come between them. Ziggy named the baby Sami, after the baby she took with her to Israel... That poor little baby got very ill once they arrived in Israel. There was not much that the hospital could do. By that time he was very sick, as he had a heart condition that was not detectable when they left. The doctors said there was not much they could do to save him but only make him comfortable.

Ziggy was heartbroken at his passing. She cried for days. After a while she settled down and spent all her time waiting to come to America. She applied for political asylum in America. She kept busy to avoid her grief. She worked as a nanny and housekeeper in Israel to survive. And then the day came to go to America. With Father Don's help she arrived in the United States safely.

* * *

And now all this happened, losing Father Don and everything. She was determined to prove her innocence and clear her good name and that of their child, Samuel. There will be a lot of gossip about this when the truth comes out.

There is a saying in Amharic that goes, "Don't hold on to the tiger's tail. If you do, never let it go or it will kill you!" Translated, it means once you decide to take action, even if it's risky, don't give up till you get to the truth! Ziggy was determined. All her setbacks and tragedy just made her stronger. Suddenly there was a knock on the door. Who could that be? She wasn't expecting anyone. Opening the door, standing right in front of her, was her cousin, NuNu, and her brother and sister. Ziggy immediately fainted on the floor. When she awoke there were many tears of joy and happiness. The long journey for her family had ended up here, in Chelsea, Massachusetts.

Ziggy prepared some food for them.

There was plenty of time to talk later. Sami woke up from his nap and was surprised to see so many people here. NuNu looked at Ziggy in surprise.

"Who's this handsome boy?" she asked.

"NuNu, this is my son, Samuel. It's a long story, and I will tell you after you have rested. Come now; let me show you to my room."

She then pulled out a cot from the closet and prepared the bed for her brother, Yonas. NuNu and her sister, Elisabeth, shared the bed. Ziggy bid them good rest and took Sami to the kitchen to feed him his lunch.

While preparing lunch, she thought of how she would proceed in finding the truth. First of all she would call Detective MacDonald and tell him the truth—on second thought, maybe not just yet. Maybe she would do a little investigating on her own first. She sat down with her little son and smiled fondly at him.

"Don't worry, baby," she said. "Mama is not going to let go of the tiger."

Sami looked up at her and laughed. "Mommy, there's no tiger here."

"Oh, I'm afraid you're mistaken, Sami, there certainly is."

Ziggy bent down and kissed him on the forehead.

* * *

Meanwhile back at the precinct, a letter came from Washington, DC, explaining that Ziggy had new representation: a defense attorney (who also specialized in immigration law) from her own country who was willing to represent her pro bono. He heard of her story from the newspaper and decided to help her in any way he could.

Actually he was related to Ziggy back home. He was a distant cousin. He knew if he didn't help her, she might not be set free.

That afternoon, Detective MacDonald called John McDevitt and explained to him the situation. John was very happy to have this off his plate.

"Thank you, Detective; I will call the new attorney this afternoon. By the way, what is his name?"

"Girma Makkonen."

Ziggy was happy to have new representation and especially someone from her country. Ziggy didn't exactly know him, but her father had. Detective MacDonald was happy about this for Ziggy. He really did not believe she murdered Father Don. He had a hunch it was someone else. Who, he was not sure. Time was moving on, and the family of Father Don was pressing for an answer, as was Father Michael.

Detective MacDonald looked at his watch and realized it was past two in the afternoon. He got into car and headed toward West Broadway. It was a nice sunny day, so he headed toward Mulligan's down by Castle Island for lunch. He found a parking spot near the front, went in, and put in his order for a cheeseburger with a side of onion rings.

"I'll have a black coffee with that," he yelled to the server. He took his meal outside and found a seat near the back of the restaurant. He enjoyed being near the water and would take a walk around the island after he finished. Out of the blue, he saw Father Michael coming around the corner finishing up his walk.

"Good afternoon, Father."

Father Michael sat down and shook Detective MacDonald's hand.

"Any news?" inquired Father Michael."

"Not yet. Ziggy has a new attorney, as you know. We've asked her to take a polygraph test. I think that may help with her defense," he said.

"It seems like you're rooting for her, Detective," Father Michael said.

"Well, if she's innocent, and I think she might be, I want her to have evidence of that. Of course, it's up to her attorney," he said. "Well, Father, I need to go. I really shouldn't be discussing a murder investigation with you, so keep it under your hat."

"You have my word, Detective," replied Father Michael.

The detective tipped his hat and said his good-bye and proceeded around the island for his walk. "I'll be talking to you soon, Father. Have a good afternoon."

"You as well, Detective." He said.

Father Michael then went into the men's room and took out a cigarette and lit up. He finished his smoke and returned to his car and headed back to the rectory. On the way back to the rectory, Father thought about what the detective said. If Ziggy was innocent, who murdered Father Don?

Father Michael was going on a two-week vacation and needed to get back to pack. He needed a rest from the stress of the home and the responsibilities of the order. He was planning to visit Father Pat at the rehab center in New York and then drive up through the Hudson Valley toward West Point. He was going to visit with his cousin, Joseph, who graduated from West Point and now lived close by in a neighboring suburb. Father Michael enjoyed the long ride there through the Hudson Valley and the serene rolling hills, which reminded him of Ireland. He enjoyed his cousin's company and was looking forward to the visit. He left Minnie in charge in his absence.

CHAPTER 14

TOM DARCY CALLED Crystal to let her know the details of the will reading. Crystal was out of the hospital and on a medical leave of absence from work. She was feeling much better now. She was reminiscing about her father and the fun times they had together as a family. Crystal's father owned a house in Bristol, New Hampshire, on Newfound Lake. They had so much fun as children. Her father was a great swimmer, as was her mother, and they would just swim and float on the lake with the kids. It was a nice memory for her and kept her in good spirits.

Crystal was busy around the house, doing her laundry and cleaning, when the phone rang.

"Hi, Crystal, it's Tom."

"How's it going, Tom?"

"Good, I just wanted to let you know the date of the will reading. It's next Wednesday at the attorney's office. You have the address?"

"I do, Tom, but I really don't want to go. It's going to make me upset, and I don't want to add to the problems I have," replied Crystal.

"That's OK, Crystal; I don't want to pressure you. I'll go and let you know what's said and see if I can get a copy of the will. If not, maybe they can reschedule in the future just for you, when you are feeling better."

"Tom, I'm sorry I yelled at you at the funeral and insulted Claire. I didn't mean it. You know how I get sometimes: whatever I think, I say," she said.

"Don't worry, Crystal. We all know that."

Tom wanted to minimize how upset Claire really was. Crystal and Claire really never got along. Crystal felt that Claire roped Tom into marrying her, and of course it proved to be true, as Tom strayed during the marriage and that was the cause of the breakup. Now they were back together and trying to give it another chance. After all, there were children involved, and Claire did not want to be divorced or even hear the word *divorce*. She went to counseling to try to deal with the infidelity, and it seemed to be working so far. Tom, on the other hand, said he was sorry, that it was a lapse in judgment, and that was it. He told Claire, "If you love me, you would forgive me. We can make things right." He refused to go to counseling, saying, "Are you crazy? You don't tell perfect strangers your innermost feelings."

Crystal felt Tom was looking out for her and did appreciate it. In reality, Tom was continuing to steal from his father's house, and with Crystal in her condition it would now be easier. He did care for Crystal, but he wanted to have what he felt was rightfully his. His father told him before his cognition declined that he wanted Tom to look out for Crystal and that he would make sure that there were provisions in the will to do this. So Tom assumed the vast majority of his father's estate would be left to him. He wasn't worried about the will reading. He was concerned, however, about any gifts that were left to Father Don and the church. Tom himself did not want anything to go to Father Don, and if it did, he would contest the will.

Father Don and Mr. Darcy were good friends, and Mr. Darcy was so grateful for the care that Father Don provided to his poor wife when she was dying of lung cancer. At that time, in his heightened state of grief, he would have given him anything to relieve the suffering his wife experienced. Margaret, Mr. Darcy's wife, was a devout Catholic. She and her husband were lay clergy in the parish and spent many years with Father Don as their pastor. There were even plans to take a trip to Medjugorje to pray for a healing. But it was too late; she passed away before the trip materialized. Mr. Darcy's health was declining at that time as well. He had Alzheimer's disease, which proved to be more advanced that anyone knew.

At the time of Margaret's passing, Mr. Darcy was in the Mansard House and unaware of her death. He had periods of lucidity, but Tom did not want to tell him of her passing, as the grief would have been too much for him to bear. He had already had a stroke, and Tom thought, why add the burden of this to his fragile condition? Father Don did not agree with this idea and confronted him about it.

"It's none of your business, Father," Tom told him. "I'm the health-care proxy for my father and have the right to make decisions on his behalf."

Father Don respected his request and backed off from the subject. Crystal had no idea her father did not know, as Tom told her not to talk about their mother or her passing to their father. Crystal did what he said. She assumed that, as her older brother, Tom was doing the right thing. She took care of her father and visited him daily. During his moments of lucidity, they reminisced about the past and the fun times they had as a family. Everyone thought Crystal didn't love her father, but she really did. The nurses knew she was looking out for his every need, and complaining was her way of taking care of him. After his passing, the nursing staff realized this about her and sent flowers and sympathy cards to the house. They knew Crystal meant well, but it didn't appear that way at times.

The day for the will reading arrived. Tom dressed carefully for the occasion in a nice suit and wing-tip shoes. He felt it was a special occasion and wanted to dress appropriately.

He went to the attorney's address in Lynnfield, Massachusetts. Tom would have preferred to have a meeting in Milton. He knew the long drive would just make him more irritable than he already was. He was very anxious about the will and really wasn't sure of the details. Now he would find out for certain. In a way, he was happy Crystal was not here to hear it. He didn't know how she would react.

As he entered the office, he noticed there was someone else in the room. Father Michael stood up and greeted him. Tom was outraged.

"Why is he here?" he yelled at his lawyer.

"Now, Tom, take it easy. Father Michael has a reason to be here. It's in your father's will that in the event that something happened to Father Don, Father Michael would be present to hear the will being read. That settled, now let me start. Just to explain, this will was amended sometime last year, exactly one year ago today."

The attorney started reading the will. Preliminary information regarding date and time and the contents of the will were described.

Then he read, "I leave the bulk of my inheritance to my sweet daughter, Crystal Darcy. The house and its contents I leave to her, the total value of which is eighteen million dollars. To my son I leave a sum of two million dollars and my Mercedes-Benz. In the event that something happens to Crystal, the inheritance will go to Tom."

Tom couldn't even speak. He could feel his blood pressure rising. Father Michael thought Tom looked as if he might faint.

"Are you OK, Tom? You're not looking too good. Can we get him a glass of water and open the window for some air?" Father asked.

His attorney moved to his side. "Take it easy, Tom. There's still more to read. Try not to get too upset."

Tom began to calm down. "I'm going to contest the will," he stated. "There is no way my father was in his right mind when he wrote that."

"Well, his signature is here and it does state that he is of sound mind and body. They even did a brief mental exam on him to make sure. We have documentation that at the time the will was drawn up, he was cognizant of what he was doing," his attorney informed him.

"I'll still contest it," Tom said. "Let's continue."

"To the Mansard House, I leave 1 million dollars to continue with the care of the residents and the retirement fund, for the clergy." Father Michael was stunned. So generous, he thought.

"To St George's church, I leave one million dollars for upkeep, maintenance costs, and for the care of the homeless."

Father Michael smiled at Tom. "Well, I had no idea, Tom, your father would leave us this sum of money. Thank you so much," he said.

"Don't thank me, Father. When I get through with this will, you and the church will not get a penny. If you think the church is going to get any of my inheritance, you are delusional. I won't give up till I get what is rightfully mine!" he screamed.

Tom stormed out of the office and slammed the door behind him. *My father was out of his mind*, he thought. *What was he thinking, leaving most of his fortune to Crystal and to the church? This is absolute nonsense.* Tom got in his car and proceeded down I-93 South Expressway toward Milton. He finally made it to his father's house. He sat in the car for a minute. He thought to himself, *I'll convince Crystal to contest it. It will look better coming from her.* He went in through the front door and greeted Crystal at the door.

He hugged Crystal and said, "I'm so happy you're doing well, Crystal. I was worried about you."

Crystal smiled and hugged Tom back.

"Oh Tom, it's so nice to know that you care about me. I thought with the way I behaved at the funeral, I might have soured our relationship."

"We're family, Crystal. We're blood. Nothing can come between us," he lied.

CHAPTER 15

ZIGGY AND NUNU sat at the kitchen table at the apartment in Chelsea. NuNu was telling Ziggy of her good fortune in receiving the lottery to come to America. She had applied for the lottery—a green card to come to America—and when she got it, she was ecstatic. She managed to get all her papers in order within a week of winning the lottery and a family member living in Kansas agreed to sponsor her. Even more coincidentally, she ran into Yonas and Elisabeth at the airport in Addis. They both had passports and papers to come to the United States. They were traveling on their own, so she immediately went with them.

"It's not safe to come all the way here being so young," she told them.

Elisabeth was seventeen and Yonas was now fourteen years old. Through the help of Father Don, a family in Dorchester had agreed to sponsor Elisabeth and Yonas to come to America. They made it through safely, with all the necessary papers in place without delay.

"It was like a miracle. I was praying to Saint Michael the whole way. I thought someone would interrogate us, but that never happened."

When they had a layover in Russia, someone did try to get money from them.

They pretended they did not speak English. They kept to themselves at the airport until the flight from Moscow was ready to resume. From there they flew all night to Washington, DC, and picked up a United Airways flight to Boston. In all, it took two days of traveling. This was a new experience for all of them. Ziggy knew they would feel this way, so she gave them a few days to rest before they were ready to talk about life in the camp after she left.

* * *

Yonas and Elisabeth now were at the kitchen table.

"Well, let me start lunch now that you two are awake. It takes a few days to feel relieved from the jetlag," Ziggy explained.

She prepared a lovely dinner for them of *wat*, *alicha*, and salad. She had just bought some Ethiopian bread, *injera*, this morning from the corner store. A lady from Arlington delivered it to the store weekly, so it was easy to get.

"Ziggy, the baby, what happened to him?" asked Elisabeth.

Ziggy told her of the sad story, how he passed away once they got to Israel.

"That's so sad, poor baby. But now you are happy again and a mother with a new baby."

Elisabeth was going to ask who the father was but refrained from asking. After all, if Ziggy wanted to tell her, she would, someday.

"I'm very happy I have a child, a healthy child."

Elisabeth nodded and went back to eating her lunch. Yonas was interested in where he would go to school; he was an excellent student who excelled in mathematics.

"I will enroll you in school soon. Don't worry, Yonas. You two will stay with me now that you are here. I will set things right with your host family."

Ziggy deliberately did not tell them of her predicament. They did notice the ankle monitor. She told them it was nothing. She said sometimes people wear security bracelets at work to locate what floor you are on, and she needed a key to take it off. They seemed to accept this explanation.

"America is very organized," Elisabeth said.

"Yes, you could say that," Ziggy replied. "Now go in the living room. You can watch television this afternoon. Listen carefully to the way people on TV speak the language. You will learn something." Ziggy then went in the bedroom to wake her son from his nap.

Later on that day, the attorney covering her case wanted to set up a time to meet with her. They set the time and place for the following week at the courthouse in Chelsea. She would be there, she promised. Did she have a choice?

The hearing was set for that week, and she insisted on pleading innocent. At least there was a trial by jury in this country, if it came to that. Ziggy felt relieved that it was a distant relative who knew her father. She had already received some funds from the Ethiopian community to help in her defense, which she would need to live on for the time being. Being held in home confinement didn't mean she could stop paying her bills. She would ask the judge if he would allow her to work while she was waiting for the trial. NuNu and Elisabeth would have to find some kind of work soon, if they were going to survive.

Girma was staying at the Holiday Inn near Logan airport. He needed to get the facts about what exactly happened to Ziggy and what evidence they had against her. He was very surprised she was arrested and put in jail. Fortunately she wasn't a flight risk so the court allowed her to be on home confinement.

Did she actually murder that priest? He didn't need to know that now, just the facts leading up to that day and the statement from the defendant. Girma had been before the court before with an Ethiopian immigrant accused of a crime. Maybe he thought he could get her off on a technicality. It didn't look good that she falsified papers to get across the border to Canada. Also, she had a child, which complicated things. She needed to work to take care of the boy.

The only one she had here was her cosponsor, Father Michael. He was a very kind man to look out for Ziggy. When Girma spoke to him, Father Michael did say if things got worse for Ziggy and she couldn't afford to live in the room she was renting, he would be able to take her and her little boy in. There were separate living quarters in the home, which she could stay in. She might be able to share a room with the housekeeper who lived in the rectory. Girma thanked him for his offer and told him he would let Ziggy know that information to reduce her worry.

The following week, Girma met Ziggy in the courthouse. He had his consultation with her in the designated conference room for clients. The children and NuNu were with her and all tried to come into the room with him.

"I'm sorry," he said, "I only need to speak with Ziggy and the rest of you need to wait in the waiting area." NuNu protested, but Girma explained this was between him and his client, and no one else was allowed to listen in. NuNu understood and took the children to the waiting area.

* * *

The hearing started and the charges were read to Ziggy and Girma.

"How does the defendant plead?" the judge said.

"Not guilty, your honor."

The judge set a date for the next hearing.

When they left the courtroom, Ziggy was feeling better.

"This is civilized, you plead not guilty, and they believe you," she said.

"Well, there's a lot more to it than meets the eye. It's all a long process, Ziggy. You have the date of the next hearing. I will be in touch with you before then. For now, we have more work to do."

Girma left the courthouse.

Ziggy, NuNu, and the children all went back to their apartment for a rest. It had been a trying day, and Ziggy was beginning to feel the strain of the whole situation. Elisabeth stared at Ziggy. *What kind of mess did she get herself into?*

CHAPTER 16

ATHER MICHAEL LEFT the attorney's office in Lynnfield and headed south on Route 1 toward the Ted Williams Tunnel, and there he picked up the Massachusetts Turnpike West exit toward New York. Father Pat was in a rehab facility in Yonkers, New York. Father Michael would stop there on his way to his cousin's house. He couldn't believe how much money was left to the Mansard House and the retirement fund.

God works in mysterious ways, he thought. He was actively praying for a miracle. The money would help a great deal to pay off some of the outstanding bills that were owed. The accountant for the house would be happy about this. Father Michael was concerned about Father Pat, and there was talk of laicization (or "defrocked," in layman's terms) from the order. He wasn't sure if he could get him out of this situation.

Father Michael, with his medical background, convinced the board that Father Pat had an addiction and needed treatment. The council would let him know of their decision soon. In the meantime he would visit to see how Father Pat was doing in his treatment.

At this point Father Michael was hoping for a suspension only. Father was making good road time through Connecticut, then on to New York. He purposely avoided the George Washington Bridge and headed toward the Tappan Zee Bridge. Fortunately there was not much traffic and he made it to the rehab center in less than five hours.

The rehab center was in a wooded area with lots of trees and open space. He saw some of the residents and counselors outside in group therapy. In another section there was a basketball court where people were playing basketball. In another area people were playing checkers. He went to the main entrance of the hospital and stopped at the front desk. There was a receptionist on the phone booking an admission. She looked up and put down the receiver.

"Can I help you, sir?" she asked.

"Yes, please, I'm here to see Father Pat O'Leary he replied.

"Are you a family member?" she asked.

"No, I'm a friend," he said.

"Can I have your name, please?"

"Father Michael O'Malley."

"OK, just a minute. You can have a seat over there, and I will have him brought down to you."

"OK, miss, thank you."

Within a few minutes, Father Pat was in the waiting room with Father Michael. They greeted each other warmly.

"How are you feeling, Father?"

"Oh I'm doing OK. It's very tiresome with all the counseling and introspection. You know me, Father Michael, I like to keep busy. I think they sent me to the wrong place. Some of the patients here are really sick. I'm not like that."

"Well, Pat, sometimes it takes a little time to realize that you have a problem. What you did was pretty outrageous, don't you think?"

"Well, I was being threatened," Father Pat said.

"Father, your gambling problem is what started this in the first place. You have some denial going on here."

"I suppose you're right, Father Michael."

"Try to use all the resources they have to offer and ask God for strength to help you throughout this difficult problem."

"Good advice, Father Michael," said Father Pat. Then he asked, "Any word from the council?"

"I'm hoping for a suspension at this point," stated Father Michael. "Stay in treatment, Father."

"I will," Father Pat replied.

"I mean it, Pat. I don't want a repeat of last time when you left against medical advice. It won't look good for you," Father Michael warned. "Well, I need to get on the road. You look well. How is the food here?"

"Very good," he replied. "They offer three meals and have an after-noon and evening snack break. Also they have an organic restaurant on-site that you can go to at minimal cost."

"Would you like to go there for supper before I leave? My treat."

"Well, aren't you the generous one," Father Pat remarked.

"We all deserve to have a nice treat for ourselves once in a while, even priests. Besides the Order has had the good fortune to inherit some money from Mr. Darcy's estate"

Father Pat looked at him. "What, the inheritance money?"

"We will talk about that later. Now I'm hungry, let's go eat."

Father Pat told the receptionist where they were going and they pro-ceeded to the Organic Garden restaurant. The restaurant was cafeteria style and self-serve, so they didn't have to wait long for their meal.

"I hope you realize you are in one of the best treatment centers in the state of New York. Also, it's very private. It's a good place for your recovery."

"How long do you think they will keep me?" Father Pat asked.

"Well, as you know, it's as long as your insurance allows. After that you can finish your sabbatical at the Friars' Monastery," Father Michael told him.

"I really miss the residents, Father. What are they going to do without me?"

"Everyone is replaceable, Father. That's a fact of life. We hired a new nurse for Mansard six. She comes with a lot of experience, and Minnie thinks she will do a good job."

"I'm not sure that's a good endorsement," Father Pat said.

"What's the problem with you two? I'm getting a negative vibe from the both of you."

"Don't get me wrong. I respect Minnie, it's just our ideas for nursing care differ a bit," he said.

"All right, Patrick, now you have my attention."

"Well, I told Minnie when we had a shortage of oxycodone for one of the patients. I thought it was sort of weird, but she told me not to worry about it and she would call the pharmacy to get more. She told me not to document it. I thought that was a violation of nursing practice," Father Pat said.

"Maybe it was nothing. We don't know the facts, but I'll check back with her when I return to the Mansard," replied Father Michael.

"Who's covering the home while you're gone, Father Michael?"

"Minnie's in charge while I'm gone."

Father Pat looked at him and rolled his eyes.

"Don't worry, Patrick. I'm sure everything is fine. I'll check in as soon as I'm settled in at my cousin Joseph's house. Don't you worry about a thing, just get better."

Father Michael and Father Pat finished their meal. Father Michael walked back to the main office and said his good-bye to Father Pat.

"You're in my prayers, Patrick."

"You're in my prayers as well, Father. Have a safe trip and a restful vacation."

"I'll return on my way back, Pat, to check in with you," Father Michael assured him.

"That will be splendid, Father."

With that, they shook hands and Father Michael gave him a quick hug and was on his way. Once he left the premises, he thought about what Father Pat had told him and was furious. He needed to stop and think for a minute. He pulled over to the side of the road to clear his head. He didn't like to drive while upset. He was too old for that and did not want to get into an accident.

What was going on with Minnie? Father Michael did not like what he heard and did not like what he was thinking. If there were a problem at the Mansard, it would not be long before it would be uncovered.

Fortunately, only Father Michael knew that the new security digital system recently installed was connected to the medication cart that required nurse identification to open. One could only access it typing in the medication, which would capture your fingerprint. The new technology was installed when they switched over to the electronic medical records. Also, new digital cameras were installed in the med rooms, which the staff were not aware of.

Father Michael put his mind to rest and proceeded onto the highway toward the Hudson Valley. He would think about all this when he returned, but for now he didn't want to jump to any conclusions. He took the next exit off the highway to travel through the small towns and scenic route. As he passed through one of the small towns, he noticed a small Irish pub, so he pulled in, parked his car, and went into the pub for a quick drink. He checked his cell phone to see if there were any messages from the home or the rectory. So far, everything seemed fine. He thought about Minnie again and then calmed down. *I'll speak to her when I return. Maybe she had a reason for what she did.* Joe, Father Michael's cousin, was waiting for him when he arrived. By this time it was past 8:00 p.m.

"Long ride," Joe said. "You must be tired, Mike. Come on in. I'll fix you something to eat and put the fireplace on. It's beginning to get cold in the evenings now. I think we might have an early fall." Then he asked, "How are you doing, Mike? You look tired."

"I'm fine, really, Joe. It's just time for a vacation. You know how it goes. Stress comes with the job. Otherwise everything is OK at the rectory." Father Michael didn't want to talk about Father Pat or any concerns that he had. "How about that golf game tomorrow? Are we still on?"

"Weather permitting," Joe said.

Father Michael and his cousin Joe finished their dinner and settled into the front living room for a nightcap.

CHAPTER 17

INNIE WAS BUSY as acting administrator while Father Michael was away. Minnie knew with the state survey approaching, everything needed to be in order and in compliance with medications, documentation, and infection control. It was better to find a mistake and try to correct it before the surveyors came and gave them a citation.

Minnie was training the new nurse, Dawn, for Mansard 6. She was working out fine and was taking notes on everything Minnie said. This was a forty-bed unit with mostly long-term dementia residents. Minnie was happy to have Dawn, who would be able to take over without much difficulty, as she had been a nurse for over twenty years. Minnie did not want to babysit any new nurses. Minnie's Parkinson's was getting worse. She was not taking the prescribed dose of Sinemet ordered for her and was in a lot of pain.

Lilian noticed this and asked if she saw the neurologist yet.

"I'm OK, Lil. The tremors and pain just go with the territory. I'll be fine. Don't worry about it. You have a busy schedule today, and there are a lot of meetings scheduled."

Minnie couldn't handle the responsibilities of the home without Father Michael there. Sure, there were other department heads about, but they all had their own workloads to handle. Minnie went into her office and locked the door. She opened her top drawer and took out two oxycodone pills. Her pain was getting unbearable. Her prescription for oxycodone was not refillable and her doctor refused to refill it till next month.

. "Minnie, I know you're taking too many of these. You're going to have a problem soon," she thought about Lilian's earlier comment. Minnie felt she could handle herself. She sat for about fifteen minutes until the pain subsided. Then she got up, unlocked the door, took her notebook, and headed to the morning medical meeting. Lillian was running the meeting this morning and was already reporting on the night shift's log. Two of the residents had passed away during the night. One had pneumonia and was frail to begin with, and the second resident was on hospice care and expired early this morning at 1:00 a.m.

Lilian did the pronouncements. She reported on a shortage of some of the meds on Mansard 6. She asked Minnie to check on this and to call the pharmacy, as this had been the third med shortage this month. Minnie said she thought maybe they could look into switching pharmacies, maybe one that would deliver sooner than the one they had. Minnie also announced that she noticed that these med errors occurred while Father Pat was on duty.

"It's just an observation," she said.

Lillian looked at her, surprised.

"Well, moving on. Next on the agenda is the new admission coming to the rehab unit. We have one new resident with a G-tube feeding. We will need to contact Jenn for a nutrition consult. The rate hasn't been set, and I want her to evaluate it. The resident has been on a bolus feeding, and I want her to evaluate for possible continuous feeding as she will probably stay here for long-term care after she finishes in rehab. Also we will need to get speech therapy involved as well. Apparently the family is bringing in food and liquids for the lady and she is NPO(Nothing passed orally). No food or liquid until further notice.

"What's her diagnosis? "Minnie asked.

"Recent stroke. She has no feeling on her left side. The patient is aphasic and has no gag reflex. We need to start monitoring fluid intake and output for the feeding and flushes. All meds are crushed and go through the tube," Lilian said.

"Are there any other issues this morning?" Lilian asked.

"Could you check on Mrs. Hurley on Mansard 3? She's running a temperature and has minimal lung sounds. She's barely eating!" the nurse manager said.

Minnie ended the meeting shortly thereafter. Lilian caught up with her and was cross.

"Minnie, why would you say that about Father Pat? Hasn't he got enough to deal with now with all his problems? I'm very surprised at you. It's so out of character and unprofessional of you."

Minnie looked at her and did not answer Lilian. She spat out, "I have work to do," and walked away.

Lilian stood there, confused.

Really, are you kidding me? She thought.

Something was wrong with Minnie and she was going to find out what it was. She had a feeling Minnie was self-medicating and that maybe the Parkinson's had gone to her brain. She would watch her over the week and consult with Father Michael when he got back. Lilian thought she might be exhibiting signs of Parkinson's dementia. Or was it something else? Only time would tell, she thought.

In the meantime Lilian was continuing to follow Ziggy's case, as were most of the staff at the Mansard. From what she heard so far, Ziggy had a new attorney that was from California but also licensed in Massachusetts to practice. Fortunate for Ziggy, she thought.

Jenn received the consult for the new tube feeding on the rehab unit. She reviewed the medical record, checked the physician's tube feeding orders, and requested to change to a continuous feeding. She started the rate slow with a recommendation to increase 25 cc daily till the goal rate was met. Jenn also noticed they did not provide enough fluids and recommended an increase each shift. She also requested weekly weights and recent labs till the resident was stabilized. The family was visiting, so she popped in to introduce herself and reviewed the importance of not feeding their mother till the speech therapist evaluated her swallowing ability. Currently the MD had ordered an MBS (modified barium study). Jenn finished documenting in the medical record and ran into Lilian on the floor. They agreed to meet in the cafeteria at 12:15 p.m. for lunch. The home was almost back to normal after the murder of Father Don. It only happened two months ago but seemed very far away now. There was a new security system in place and alarms on all the doors on the outside and inside.

Father Michael hired a new security team that had four more security guards on staff. There was a drug problem in the neighborhood. Being a large facility, it could become a target. Jenn looked at the watch her husband gave her for her birthday and checked the time. She headed toward the cafeteria to meet up with Lilian.

Lilian had not arrived yet, so Jenn got a seat and pulled out her knitting from her bag. She was working on a baby blanket for her oldest daughter, Lois, as she was expecting a new baby. They weren't sure of the sex, so she was making it with rainbow colors. Jenn couldn't wait to be a grandmother. She knew if Lois was pregnant, her other daughter, Liana, would be pregnant soon as well. Liana always followed in her oldest sister's footsteps. Liana was living in Toronto and working as a buyer for a large retail company in Canada. Her other daughter, Lauren, was a pediatric nurse in the ICU at a Hospital in Boston. She worked in the high-risk nursery with the premature babies. She was very smart and planned on going to medical school in the future. She was taking the MCAT in the fall. Jenn was very proud of her girls. She had recently returned from her vacation in Maine with the whole family. The boys were doing well also. Jed was finishing up his college degree and looking for an apartment with one of his college roommates. Her son, Jeffrey, was getting married soon. Jenn thought about the dresses hanging in her closet from both of her daughter's recent weddings. In her closet, a midlength navy-blue dress with sparkles and a shrug jacket still had the tags on it. She would wear it to Jeffrey's wedding, she thought.

Jenn looked up from her daydreaming and saw Lilian approaching with her lunch tray.

"Busy day, huh?" Lilian sighed.

"Yeah, pretty busy for me. Three consults so far so, and I haven't finished the assessments due today," Jenn said. Lilian told Jenn about their medical meeting this morning and how she was worried about Minnie. Jenn knew Minnie had Parkinson's, as Minnie often came by her office to talk about diet recommendations regarding adjusting the protein intake with the medication. She knew Minnie's tremors were bad; she noticed them when Minnie was holding the telephone receiver one day while answering an overhead page.

"Well, what can you do, Lilian? Father Michael will be back from his vacation soon, and you can talk to him when he returns. You can't force someone to go back to the doctor. She'll figure it out. She's a smart woman. All you can do is be there if she needs someone to talk to."

Lilian agreed with Jenn, and they continued with their lunch. Lilian didn't tell Jenn about her suspicions that she was over medicating herself and that maybe the Parkinson's was affecting her brain. She would keep her eye on Minnie for any new symptoms and decide what to do from there.

Suddenly there was an overhead page for Lilian. "Stat! Mansard six!" Lilian rushed to the floor as the other nurses grabbed the crash cart. Minnie had collapsed on the floor while checking the med cart. Lilian checked her vital signs. Her blood pressure had dropped and her respirations were slow.

Minnie felt cold and clammy to her. "Call 911, fast!" she yelled. "I need some oxygen here!"

Immediately the floor nurse was there with a cannula and portable oxygen tank. With the oxygen flowing, Minnie started to regain consciousness. She looked at Lilian and smiled.

"You're going to be OK, Minnie, we called 911. The ambulance should be here in a minute."

Minnie gave Lilian a faint smile and held on to her hand as the paramedics arrived on the floor.

CHAPTER 18

CRYSTAL WAS SO happy with the news of her inheritance. She thought she might have to move but was happy she didn't have to. She was a little surprised Tom didn't get more of the settlement and felt maybe it was a mistake on her father's part. Under the Family Protection Act, Tom could contest the will as he saw fit. Crystal agreed with him, and the proceedings had already started.

Being a paralegal, Crystal knew this information after she consulted with the law firm. Tom, on the other hand, wanted also to contest any settlement that was left to the church and the friars' retirement fund. Tom felt his father was in an advanced state of dementia when he rewrote his will. This would hold up the funds until a decision was made. The attorney for the will reading was also the executor of the estate.

Funeral expenses and debts to the Mansard House for her father's care were already distributed as allowed. Crystal was planning on having an appraiser evaluate the net worth of everything that was left to her. There was her father's art collection, antique furniture, and extensive jewelry collection of her mother's, not to mention investments. Claire, Tom's wife, was very upset about what Tom received and also felt it was unfair. Claire never liked Mr. Darcy or Crystal, for that matter, and she really didn't care how Tom manipulated Crystal, as long as he secured more of the inheritance.

Crystal, being good natured and trusting, was already thinking of splitting everything in half, except the home, to compensate Tom. Claire thought this was a great idea, but she also thought Crystal was naive in her dealings with Tom. It was easy to take advantage of her with her recent mental breakdown and vulnerability.

Claire knew that Tom had a lot of his father's belongings in the cedar chest in the cellar, even though he didn't know she knew. She found his key to the chest and made a copy of it when he was at work. She opened the chest and was amazed at how much was in there. She never let Tom know she was aware of this. In fact, she thought he might have committed grand larceny. If she was ever called into a court of law, she would never admit to any knowledge of this. She did not want any part of Tom's actions, but she was also not going to call the police.

In the meantime, Crystal arranged for an appraiser to come to the house next week. She wanted to keep records of everything and her net worth. Tom wanted her to wait, but Crystal insisted on continuing with the appraisal. Tom was a little concerned about what the appraiser would find. He knew the paintings were replaced with imitations, but they were so detailed it would take an art dealer to examine it closely to figure it out. In the meantime, Tom stayed close to his father's house and checked up on Crystal frequently. He wanted to take more things from the house before she had everything inventoried. Crystal was so gullible, he thought.

Crystal was finally feeling better after her hospitalization and had returned to work full-time. The attorney that she worked for wanted her to sit in on a case in their conference room as a witness to signing legal papers. As she was about to enter the conference room, she saw a familiar face.

"How are you doing, Ms. Darcy? I had no idea you worked in this law firm. I'm so sorry to hear of your fathers passing," he said.

Crystal looked at him and suddenly recalled who he was, John McDevitt, counsel for the Mansard Corporation. "Oh thank you, Mr. McDevitt, I appreciate that. What is your business here today with us?" Crystal responded. She couldn't help notice how handsome John was outside of the nursing home environment, and that he dressed very well.

Her boss suddenly appeared and carried on with the proceedings. Crystal couldn't stop glancing at John and noticing his beautiful green eyes. Mr. McDevitt had the same trouble concentrating. He noticed how poised and professional Crystal was and that she wasn't wearing a wedding band.

After the meeting he came up to her to say good-bye and asked if she would like to go out for some coffee. Crystal was so thrilled. She hadn't dated in a long time and immediately agreed.

"I noticed there was a bistro a block down the street. Maybe we could get a sandwich. Have you eaten your lunch?" he asked.

"That's sounds great. Let me finish up my work and we can leave together," she said.

Crystal finished up her report while John waited, talking with her boss. Apparently they went to law school together.

"All set," Crystal interrupted.

They both left the office and took the elevator to the first floor. They walked a few blocks down Milk Street and found the bistro on the corner. It was busy, but they managed to find a cozy booth and stayed an extra fifteen minutes while sipping their coffee and finishing up their dessert.

"Well, I must get back to work. That was lovely. Thanks so much for asking me to lunch," Crystal said sincerely.

"Crystal, I enjoyed myself, thank you," he said. Crystal gave him a smile and started walking back to the office.

"Crystal, I'm going in the opposite direction, my car is parked two streets over, but I was wondering if you would like to have dinner with me on Friday night?" he asked expectantly.

"Absolutely, I'd love to." Crystal gave him her cell phone number.

John said he would call her later after she got home tonight. They said their good-byes and Crystal went back to work. She had a bounce in her step and was humming as she entered the office. For the rest of the afternoon, Crystal was thinking how nice John McDevitt was and what a coincidence to meet him here. *My good fortune*, she thought.

Friday came soon enough and they went to an upscale restaurant in Cambridge.

The lights were dim and the sound of a jazz ensemble flowed easily through the air as they sat by the window, looking out to the Charles River. The boats were lined up and the cool breeze of the evening blew her hair into the muted light.

"This is so quaint. Look at the small café tables and beautiful tablecloths. It feels like you're in a French café in Paris," Crystal said.

"I've been here a few times and have enjoyed the smell of the food cooking," John said.

Just then the waiter approached. "May I get you a bottle of wine before you order?" he asked.

"Wine would be great. Is that OK with you, Crystal?" He did not want to presume she drank wine. John ordered the wine in French and ordered dinner for them both.

After dinner, Crystal said to the waiter, "The duck was delicious and cooked the way I like it. My compliments to the chef." Being a student of the skill, she understood the care it took to prepare the meal. The waiter left the table and returned to the kitchen.

* * *

"I had a wonderful time, Crystal," he said.

"I did, too, John. What a great restaurant. So romantic and you speak French fluently. I'm so impressed."

"Oh, don't be. I had to learn French for my work since we deal with a lot of foreign investors."

"Oh, I see," said Crystal. Soon they arrived back at Crystal's place.

John leaned forward into Crystal and kissed her. She kissed him back. They stayed on the door step for a while. Crystal felt like a young girl on her first date. Crystal went into the house and waved out the window as John drove away in his Acura. She hadn't felt this happy in a long time.

The phone rang; it was Tom.

"Crystal, where have you been? I've been calling you all night!"

"Oh, I'm sorry Tom. I turned off my cell phone. "

"Where were you?" he asked.

"I had a date, Tom."

"With whom?" Tom asked, surprised.

"I went out with John McDevitt, you know, the attorney for the Mansard House."

"Oh." Tom was stunned. "Crystal, I'll drop by tomorrow then."

"I'm sorry, Tom, but I'll be gone for most of the day. I'll catch up with you on Sunday. See you. I've got to go. Talk to you later," Crystal exclaimed.

Tom sat in his living room with the receiver in his hand. She hung up so quickly, Tom didn't even have a chance to say good-bye.

CHAPTER 19

THE SECOND HEARING for Ziggy was tomorrow. Girma called Ziggy to confirm the time for the hearing. It was very important that she not be late. He told her it was better if she came without the children. Ziggy met Girma at the courthouse. They went into the client /attorney conference room and discussed the possibility that the case would be thrown out for insufficient evidence. They both entered the courtroom and waited for their hearing to come up.

An hour had passed as other hearings were in progress. Ziggy thought they would never call her case and began to feel anxious.

Then she heard it. The prosecutor presented her case with the alleged evidence.

After the prosecutor presented his case, Girma requested to have the case thrown out for insufficient evidence. He also demanded to dismiss the case because the Miranda rights were not read to her. The judge heard the arguments from the attorneys and finally made his statement.

"In the case of Ziggy Tena, the state of Massachusetts dismisses her case for lack of sufficient evidence and violation of her civil rights."

He hit the gavel and declared the case dismissed and the defendant was free to go. Ziggy and Girma stayed on to sign some documents and remove the ankle security alarm and then left the courthouse. After leaving court they ran into Detective MacDonald.

"Congratulations, Ziggy. It seems you are cleared of any wrongdoing," he remarked.

"Thank you, Detective."

Detective MacDonald looked down and noticed a small ring on her left hand.

Ziggy told him that Father Don was Sami's father and that their son now would have his mother back to raise him, instead of being in jail.

Detective MacDonald was stunned. He didn't have any words to say. Finally after a minute of silence to regain his composure, he spoke.

"Ziggy, I had no idea. Does Father Michael know?" he asked.

"He knows. Don told him." She didn't offer any further explanation.

Now the investigation would continue. So far, two months had passed without much more evidence. Detective MacDonald was shocked at her admission that Father Don was in fact her lover and the child was their offspring. *Women do kill their lovers* he thought. Isn't the partner usually a suspect? In Ziggy's case he knew in his heart; call it a hunch, that she didn't do it. But who did? That was the question. Detective MacDonald was reviewing the facts in his head when his cell phone rang. His officer let him know of the recent reading of Mr. Darcy's will. The fact that the church and the retirement fund received a large sum of money meant that the son, Tom, was probably contesting the will. Also, his officer told him, the bulk of the money and the estate went to his daughter, Crystal.

Detective MacDonald was wondering how the brother was taking this. He knew Tom had a temper, and he witnessed it firsthand while interrogating him for the murder of Father Don. Tom denied any wrongdoing and hired a fancy attorney to keep him at bay. Detective MacDonald knew something wasn't making sense. Clues were missing. He might take a second look at the crime scene again at the Mansard. *Yes*, he thought to himself, *that is what we will do. Start over.*

It appeared that Tom did keep tabs on Father Don's whereabouts, as was evident by his cell phone records. He was sure all that talk was not of a spiritual nature. Mr. Tom Darcy was still on Detective MacDonald's radar. He had a suspicion he was up to no good. Call it a detective's hunch.

Ziggy thanked Girma for all his assistance and invited him back to her home to have some dinner before he returned to the hotel. Girma thanked her but regretfully had to fly back to California that night. His wife would pick him up at the airport and he was anxious to get home. He was very happy Ziggy was let go and that she would be free to pursue her dreams and raise her child. He felt very bad for her, not having a husband and all the suffering she had endured to get to this country. He couldn't believe how strong a woman she was, and he admired her. He knew she would be OK now and would stay here in this country with her brother, sister, and her child. She had a good head on her shoulders and was practical. She could put the past behind her and move forward.

Ziggy said her good-bye to Girma and wished him and his family well. She would tell her family what he did for her and how he came to her rescue. She would not forget his kindness and understanding. Ziggy walked up to the second-floor apartment and heard her brother and sister in the house, preparing lunch and talking. She did not say too much about what happened, because she never told her cousin or her brother and sister about all the trouble she had been in. She also never revealed who the father of her child was and never intended to. She would keep that part of her life to herself. She sat with her family at the kitchen table. She prepared some coffee and set out the coffee cups for her and her cousin NuNu. The mail had arrived early that afternoon and she saw it on the nearby counter.

It was from UMass Boston. Ziggy pulled open the envelope. Inside was her acceptance letter as a transfer student to begin as a junior in the department of health sciences. Most of her credits were accepted from Addis Ababa University. There were some classes that had to be taken before she would be accepted into the nursing program. They would help her with any problems she had with the class schedule. Now she could get a good job and take care of her family. She was very happy today to be cleared of any wrongdoing and to move forward in her life.

In the meantime Elisabeth and Yonas were enrolled in school. Elisabeth and Yonas attended Chelsea High School. Ziggy enrolled them both into an afterschool group for foreign students of all nationalities. The afterschool group would assist them with their homework and English practice, which would be necessary for both of them. Now that Ziggy was deemed innocent and did not have a criminal record, she decided that first thing in the morning she would start to apply for a nurse's aide position. In fact, while she was in the courthouse, she noticed in the local neighborhood paper an advertisement seeking nurse's aides for a nursing home in Chelsea. She would apply first thing Monday morning.

Ziggy put all this behind her. But Elisabeth had other ideas in mind. She hadn't been with Ziggy for many years now and felt she was an independent person now that she was in America and wanted to assimi-late into the society as much as she could. Yonas, on the other hand, was still very young and would need to stay with Ziggy for a while until he finished high school. Elisabeth was a senior and was planning on moving out to college as soon as the year was out. *Ziggy is not the only one who can keep a secret*, she thought.

The next day, Ziggy sent her résumé to the job she saw in the paper. She hoped they would call for an interview. She already met with the host family that sponsored her brother and sister to thank them and let them know her siblings would now be living with her. NuNu had already left and moved to Kansas where her sponsor family lived. It was time for Ziggy to move on with her life.

CHAPTER 20

LILIAN ENTERED THE hospital room where Minnie was admitted. She didn't look good. Her tremors were coming on full force, and they had her on oxygen. Lilian entered and sat by her bed. Minnie roused from her sleep and gave a faint smile.

"How are you feeling?" asked Lilian

"Like a fool," Minnie groaned.

"You collapsed, Minnie. It was probably from the Parkinson's and taking too much pain medication."

"Yeah, that's what the doctor said," she replied. "The neurologist will be coming by in the morning. They have already increased my dose of Sinemet. They want me to stay till I'm stabilized and on the right medications.

"I really have been a fool, Lilian. I know I have been trying to handle everything and have been in denial about my illness."

"Well, you're not perfect, Minnie, and you're not alone. A lot of people try alternative routes, so don't beat yourself up. Just get well and get some rest. I'll come by again in a few days to see how you're doing. In the meantime, one of the other friars from the rectory will take over until Father Michael comes back. I'll cover what needs to be done in the nursing department."

"You're an angel, Lilian." Minnie sighed.

"I'll talk to you soon."

Lilian left the room, but not before talking to Minnie's nurse. "How is she doing?" she asked.

"She's better than when she first came in. She took too much oxyco-done. The doctor wants to make sure she doesn't take it again and wants to keep her till she weans off. She's addicted to it. She keeps asking for it, but they're giving her acetaminophen for pain. We see this a lot. The more you use, the more you need. It's hard to stop it on your own."

"Has anyone else been in to visit?" Lilian asked.

"Just her family and a friend, I think it's her roommate," the nurse said.

Lilian said good-bye to the nurse and headed out toward her car.

While she was leaving she spotted Detective MacDonald in the lobby of the hospital. *I wonder what he is doing here,* she thought. *I hope he is not going to question Minnie. She will be really upset if she sees him. She never cared for Detective MacDonald, and in her condition she might say something offensive, although it's hard to offend the detective.*

Detective MacDonald was retracing his steps in the murder investigation to see if he missed anything. With Ziggy out of the picture as a suspect, he was interviewing everyone at the home again. What did he miss? During his last conversation with Minnie, she never really said how well she knew the victim, or if she knew him at all. At the time of their interview, the investigation was centered on Ziggy as the prime suspect. Not anymore.

Through Officer Ed he learned Minnie had a drug overdose and was being treated here at Massachusetts Memorial Hospital. Why was she using drugs and especially oxycodone? He would have to get to the bottom of this. Maybe it was nothing, no connection to the murder of Father Don, but one never knew. Crimes had a way of revealing themselves. He just had to start back at the beginning.

He knew he would have trouble with retrieving information from Lilian, as she was strict about her policy of privacy, especially medical information. *Well, I'm going to find a way around it,* he thought to himself. It was time to make another visit to Father Michael. Detective MacDonald left the hospital and decided to question Minnie at another time. He recalled she was quick to get rid of him last time and was relieved at the idea that Ziggy was the prime suspect. As a matter of fact, she went around announcing it to everyone. It had been two months now and there really weren't any other breaks in the case.

The judge threw out the fingerprints evidence because there were multiple prints on the alleged murder weapon, not just Ziggy's. He had confirmed insufficient evidence. Now with Ziggy's revelation that Father Don and she were more than just friends, Ziggy's behavior made sense: first at the funeral mass and then leaving town with their child to start a new life in Canada. Who could blame her for being paranoid after all she had endured? Falsely accused in her own country, and then coming here to America and being accused of murder? *I knew why she told me*, the detective thought, *to clear her good name.*

Detective MacDonald had a few other suspects in mind and was determined to find out who the murderer was. Detective MacDonald left MMH and headed downtown. It was getting near supper time, and he and Officer Ed were in the mood for Chinese food. They went to Chinatown and ducked into a Chinese restaurant on the corner of Washington Street near Tufts Medical Center.

Rain was in the forecast and it started to pour. They parked close by, luckily, before the rain started. They both sat at a table in the window, which was decorated with Chinese lanterns and a Buddha display. The restaurant was packed with shoppers coming in from China town. The cement dragons on the staircase stared back at them. MacDonald ordered a Sam Adams and lit up a cigarette. The smoke floated across the window, and raindrops pounded on the windowpane. The waiter came and they ordered the PuPu Platter for two with a side of fried rice.

They ordered a second round of beers. Father Michael would be back from his vacation soon, and Detective MacDonald would pay him a visit. The food finally came, and both he and the officer sitting in their booth, didn't speak again till they'd eaten the last of the pork strips.

CHAPTER 21

CRYSTAL WAS JUST getting up on Sunday morning, after her late night with John. It was eleven o'clock, and she felt no guilt about sleeping in. During the weekday she was usually up at six and out the door by seven to make it to downtown Boston by eight. Traffic was always bad in the morning. If you didn't leave early enough, the 93 South Expressway would be in a gridlock.

Someone was knocking on the front door. Crystal first put her water and coffee pod into the new coffee machine and then went to answer the front door. Someone was persistent. She stepped down onto the front porch to open the front screen door. It was Tom.

"Crystal, why aren't my keys working?" he asked.

"Oh, I had the locks changed, Tom," she said.

"Why would you do that?" His temper was rising.

"I just thought it was a good idea, since the house is mine. You can come by anytime you want, Tom, just let me know and I'll make sure I'm home."

"Where did you get that idea from, your new boyfriend?" he said.

"I was thinking of it anyway. There were a few sets of keys around, and I couldn't locate them all. With Dad's passing, I could never find his set, so I thought it might be safer to change the locks. Don't you think it's a good idea?" Crystal tried to persuade him.

"I guess so," Tom said reluctantly. "The only one I'm concerned about is you, Crystal. What if you got sick again? How would I get into the house if you needed help?" he lied.

"Oh Tom, always the worrier," she said sweetly. "I'll get a set made for you if you're that concerned."

"I think that would be the smart thing to do," he said. *Smart for me*, he thought. "How was your date last night with Counselor McDevitt?"

"His name is John, Tom. Be nice. I really like him, he's a good guy, and we have a lot in common. It's been a while since I've been with someone I really like. That doesn't happen that easily for me. I'm not as outgoing as you are, Tom," she said introspectively. "Maybe we could all go out sometime together."

"I'll ask Claire, maybe we can. Don't you think it's a coincidence that you met him just when you received millions of dollars in your father's will?"

"I think it's just what it is, a random coincidence, that's all. I don't want to think the worst of people just because I inherited Daddy's money."

"All right, Crystal. Be optimistic, I'm just warning you, that's all," he said.

"I think we need to get off the subject and have something to eat. Do you want a late breakfast, Tom? I was just going to make an omelet for myself, and I have some blueberry muffins I baked yesterday. The coffee is ready. I'll make you a cup in my new coffee pod machine. It's great. It will only take five minutes."

"OK, Crystal, I'll stay for breakfast. I'm just going to wash up upstairs in Mom's old bathroom," he said.

"OK. I'll be in the kitchen. Come down when you're ready."

Tom took the backpack with him upstairs. He could hear Crystal in the kitchen listening to music and singing softly to herself. He went into the bathroom and turned the sink faucet on as if he was washing his hands. He then went into his parents' bedroom and into the jewelry chest on the side of the bureau.

He opened the chest and took out his mother's watches and gemstone rings and placed them in the backpack. He went into his father's top drawer and found the combination to the wall safe. He copied down the number and planned to return when he had more time.

Just then as he was leaving the bedroom, Crystal was climbing the stairs. She didn't see him leave his parents' bedroom. He slipped into the bathroom and turned the faucet off just as she made it to the top of the stairs.

"Come down for breakfast, Tom. Everything's ready. Come now, while the food is hot. I think you will enjoy it," she said.

Tom walked down behind her and sat at the kitchen table while she served him breakfast. Tom left soon after breakfast to go to the gym for his workout. He had been to this gym before and found the trainer, Heidi, very attentive. He headed toward Braintree to the South Shore Athletic Club. He had been working out there for the past month. He arrived at the gym and entered the weight room. He saw Heidi with a client and she waved to him as he came in.

In the meantime Claire was calling on his cellphone. Tom answered.

"Hi, Claire," he said.

"I thought we could grab an early supper and catch a movie tonight. What do you think?"

"Well,. I should be back home about four o'clock. Is that OK with you?" he said.

"That's great," she said. "I'm going to get a pedicure, so I will see you later."

"It's a date!" Tom said, and he hung up the phone.

Claire was so happy that things were working out since they got back together. Tom was really trying, she thought. She hurried on to the spa and thought about what outfit she could wear for their "date." Tom waved back to Heidi. As she approached, Tom sucked in his gut and flexed his biceps.

"Looking good," Heidi said. "Keep up the good work."

"Are you my trainer for the day?" he asked.

"Oh no," she said. "Jim will be working with you. I'm leaving early to meet my fiancé." Heidi beamed.

Tom nodded his head and took a deep breath.

Jim approached him and asked, "Are you ready for some sit-ups?"

"I'm actually feeling a little tired today. I'll just work out on my own, thanks, Jim," he said.

"Suit yourself. We are here if you need any assistance."

Tom completed his work out in thirty minutes.

He headed to the exit and recognized one of Claire's gossipy friends.

"Hi, Tom, I didn't know you worked out here," Monica said.

"Why don't you come out with Claire, and I'll drag Charlie with me? He could certainly use it. Tell Claire I said hello," she said.

Oh great, Tom thought, *now she'll tell Claire she saw me at this gym, and she'll question me endlessly.* She was very suspicious of him.

"OK, Monica that sounds good. See you later now." He headed toward the men's shower and spotted Heidi with her fiancé embracing in the corner.

CHAPTER 22

FATHER MICHAEL WAS on his return trip from his cousin's home. He really enjoyed playing golf and swimming at his cousin's summer house. His cousin had four children, two boys and two girls. The girls were both married and both had children. His sons were both at the Military Academy at West Point, following in their father's footsteps. One was graduating this year and the other was a sophomore.

Father Michael and Joe went to visit them. They attended Mass in their stained-glass chapel and met in Grant Hall afterward to chat and decide where to go for their dinner. They spent their day walking around the grounds and discussing how much the academy had changed. Women were now allowed and they passed many female cadets on their tour. Joseph was a good father and the children were very respectful of their parents. His wife, Mary, was very sweet and worked as a high school teacher right near West Point. Father Michael's vacation had come to an end, and he said good-bye to his cousin and his family. He drove south toward the rehab center in Yonkers. He stopped off to see Father Pat on his return, just as he promised.

What a change in two weeks. Father Pat was doing very well and apparently had settled into the program and what it had to offer. They asked him to say Mass at the chapel there and provide pastoral counseling for the young teen groups. Father Pat revealed he found this very rewarding and found camaraderie with some of the other patients that had the same problems. Father Michael was very happy he was adjusting. They met for a short visit, and then he was off, back on the highway home to Massachusetts.

He called the rectory and talked to Father Paul. He was covering for him since Minnie was in the hospital. Father Paul told Father Michael the situation. Father Michael was very surprised to hear she had collapsed on the floor.

"Minnie needs to get her condition under control. I think it's time to let her go," he said to Father Paul. With the story of the oxycodone being missing and her behavior changes, Father Michael thought maybe the Parkinson's was advancing. He couldn't prove it, but he had his suspicions that Minnie might be stealing the oxycodone from the med cart. There were certainly many opportunities to do it. He would check back on the security system to see if this had already happened.

Unfortunately, her actions had legal consequences.

He decided to let Minnie go and had already contacted the personnel department to do this. He could offer her a severance package for her service. If there were any questions, Father Michael would seek to press charges. That was it. There was nothing more he could do. His main allegiance was to the Mansard House and its residents. He would ask personnel to post an ad in the paper this weekend for a director of nursing. He felt bad about this, but these decisions came with the territory. Minnie should apply for disability, but that was her decision, and she needed to figure it out.

Father Michael was making good time on the highway. He just made it through Connecticut and was entering the Massachusetts border. He was getting tired and it was a long ride. He pulled over to the next rest stop for food and took a supper break. He ordered a slice of vegetable pizza and a hot cup of coffee. He stayed at the food court for about twenty minutes and then returned to the highway. Soon he was on the Massachusetts Turnpike, headed toward Boston. He finally got off at the Albany Street exit and then drove over the Broadway Bridge and into South Boston. He was happy to be home. Father parked his car and Father Paul met him at the door. After he freshened up, they sat at the kitchen table sipping a cup of Dublin tea together. Father Paul did a great job covering the home and handling all the turmoil that arose. Father Michael decided to make him the assistant administrator. He knew when he needed help, and with the situation with Minnie, having Father Paul as the assistant administrator would provide greater coverage until a new director was hired.

Father Michael excused himself and went to his room. He wanted to get a good night's rest to be prepared to handle the next day. He didn't like uncomfortable situations, but it had to be done.

* * *

Minnie was now at her house, recovering from her hospitalization. Her meds had been adjusted and her doctor had her in an outpatient program to withdraw from the oxycodone. Father Michael called her and asked how she was feeling. He said to come by to his office that afternoon. Minnie drove herself to the Mansard. She knew what was coming and decided to resign from her position. She met with Father Michael, who reviewed the events that occurred and accepted her resignation. He decided not to take legal action against Minnie, as they were friends and he understood her predicament. He felt partially responsible by allowing her to smoke marijuana in the home and should have stopped this earlier. Father Michael walked her to the front door and bid her well. Minnie thanked him for his kindness.

"I'll keep you in my prayers, Minnie."

"Thanks, Father," she said. "I'm going to need them."

She left soon after that and said Lilian would return her things from her office. She was embarrassed by her behavior and did not want to stay around too long.

The director of nurses position was posted in the *Boston Globe* over the weekend. Monday morning they had received over ten resumes. Jobs were tight in health care with all the downsizing and cutbacks in the hospitals and nursing home closings. Father Michael wanted personnel to handle this and asked Lilian to be involved. One person who stood out was a nurse with twenty years of experience as a nursing manager. He was let go from his job two months ago after downsizing. Lilian called him in for an interview and was impressed with all his experience, especially in acute care and geriatrics. All his references had glowing reports about his professionalism and ability to deal with other departments and work as a team player.

Father Michael interviewed him as well and agreed he was the best choice of all the candidates that applied. Personnel offered him the position and he readily agreed. Lilian liked the fact that he had teaching experience and did work as a nurse educator.

This would help a lot with the new graduate nurses recently hired. Father Michael felt relieved that the position was filled and that Steve was such an affable and warm person. The last thing he wanted was to have someone who was removed from the nurses and just a figurehead. Steve was very involved with the staff and did daily rounds with Father Michael to get to know all the residents and the nurses working on the floors. Steve appeared very professional on the job and did not bring any of his personal problems to work. His philosophy was when you entered the facility to do your job, you left your personal problems on the doorstep outside. Lilian liked that about him. In the meantime Father Paul was training to be the assistant administrator and was shadowing Father Michael as well. He enjoyed all the administrative training, much to his surprise.

Father Paul was an accountant for a big firm before he entered the order so he was happy to use his skills in helping with the budget for the home. Father Paul also ran the household budget with the other friars. Things were beginning to calm down at the Mansard House and settle back into a routine again till Detective MacDonald called again one morning.

"Father Michael, I just wanted to give you an update on the investigation so far. As you know, Ziggy Tena was cleared of all wrongdoing, as most of the evidence was insufficient. Also she passed the polygraph. Needless to say, we are retracing our steps and want to reexamine all the facts so far in the case. I would like your permission to examine the crime scene again and see if there is any small detail we may have missed."

Father Michael agreed. He was just as anxious to find Father Don's murderer, as was everyone else at the home. The resident residing in the room previously occupied by Mr. Darcy and the murder victim was moved to another floor. The floor was being renovated, so it was a good time for the detective to investigate. Detective MacDonald would start the next day with looking farther than the room for any clues. This time they would use luminol to see if they had missed any bloodstains in the room or in the nearby vicinity. Father Michael wanted to downplay the investigation. He did not discuss this with his staff and allowed Detective MacDonald full access to the floor. He did ask him not to use the crime scene tape so as not to alarm the residents.

The following morning they arrived with a full homicide team. They began spraying the room with luminol. Nothing much came off the walls, just fingerprints. Out in the hallway was a large tub room and shower area. They sprayed the luminol on all the walls and were shocked at what they found. The luminol revealed bloodstains all across the walls and near the tub. It looked like there was a struggle and that Father Don put up a fight. Detective MacDonald stood with his mouth open in shock.

"Well, I'll be damned, look at all this blood."

He got on the cell phone and called it into the team to get a bloodstain analyst over there immediately. It would take a few days to get all the facts from this finding. He continued to look around and found an old hamper. He opened the hamper and to his surprise was a bloodstained towel. This must have been used to clean up the mess. The fact that Father Don may have been murdered in the tub room and then have his body dragged all the way to Mr. Darcy's room evoked some serious questions. Why did it matter to anyone where the body would be found? Only, he thought, if the perpetrator was trying to set up the scene and make it look like Father Don was murdered in the resident's room. The fact that Ziggy was Mr. Darcy's full-time aide made it clear to him that someone might have been trying to frame Ziggy all along. What about the murder weapon? Was the knife actually the weapon that caused such a large amount of blood on the wall? He would call Matt in the coroner's office tomorrow to reexamine the coroner's report. Something was fishy here. His gut feelings were telling him that the knife in their possession was not the murder weapon. Call it a premonition. He just had a feeling.

CHAPTER 23

ZIGGY HEARD FROM the position at the nursing home in Chelsea. They wanted to hire her right away, as they were desperate for help. She accepted the position, which was full-time and provided full benefits. *What a godsend*, she thought. *God is shining his grace on me.* Elisabeth and Yonas were all settled in the high school. The host parents from Dorchester were still involved in their lives, and they would go over on Sundays for dinner. They wanted to make sure things were going as Father Don had arranged. Elisabeth was meeting other teenagers her own age and was making friends. She was asking to go out with her friends more in the evening, and Ziggy didn't know if she liked that idea.

There were some Ethiopian students that she met, too, and they would meet up to get their hair done or go shopping. Ziggy thought it would be a good idea for Elisabeth to get a part-time job and work at the nursing home with her. She inquired about this and Elisabeth was hired to work in the kitchen as long as she could get working papers. Ziggy was happy about this. Elisabeth would ask her for money often. Elisabeth needed her own money, and this way Ziggy could also keep an eye on her.

Yonas was very reliable and very interested in school. After school he had joined the math club and the chess club just to have some fun. He was fascinated by chess and advanced very rapidly with the other players. They were amazed at how quick he was to grasp the strategies in playing chess. Little Sami was now in preschool. He attended the preschool right next to the high school. Elisabeth would drop him off in the morning and

Ziggy would pick him up at three o'clock, right after her shift. They were settling into a normal life in America and putting the past behind them.

One night they attended an international dance festival at the convention center in the Seaport District in Boston. There were so many people there and many new faces. They had food from different countries, and people were dancing the *eskista* from her country.

She was on the side sitting and NuNu was dancing with her sister when someone cut in to dance with them. Here right in front of her was her old running partner, Daniel, from Ethiopia.

She was so surprised and could not believe Daniel was here. "Daniel!" she yelled. She had not seen him since her days as a student.

"Ziggy," he said, "I can't believe it's you." They hugged each other warmly.

Elisabeth, Yonas, and Sami came over to see what the commotion was about. Ziggy introduced her family and they all sat down and ate their dinner together. Daniel, like NuNu, had won the lottery to come to this country. He was also living in Chelsea with his brother. Daniel had studied to become a pharmacist and was back in school now to complete the required courses to become a pharmacist in America. It had been many years since Daniel had seen Ziggy, but he was happy to see that she was well and had a child. He didn't know if she was married. He did not see a wedding band. *Time will tell what her story is*, he thought. He knew he did not want to lose her. He noticed she was dressed in black. He knew this meant she might be in mourning, as was the traditional way.

Ziggy made plans to meet with Daniel for coffee the next day. They had a lot to catch up on. The evening had ended, and Ziggy gave a small bow to say good-bye. *She's still beautiful with her almond eyes and lovely smile*, he thought. *I'm not going to let her out of my sight. Never again.* He smiled back and said good night to the whole family.

Ziggy's heart ached when she saw him. She felt this way at home. She never thought she would ever see Daniel again in her lifetime. Now he was here. *What does God have in store for me?* She waved back to him as they entered the train station on their way back to Chelsea.

Ziggy was putting the past behind her. She decided it was time to sever her relationship from Father Michael and the home as it was all a painful reminder of Father Don. It was time to move on.

CHAPTER 24

I T WAS EARLY Sunday morning and Detective MacDonald was up with the birds as usual. He was on his second cup of coffee and already had a toasted bagel with a mound of cream cheese on it. He liked cream cheese, especially the kind with chives and onion. He opened his basement cellar door and took his cigarettes with him. His painting supplies and canvas were ready for him.

His wife, Margie, was still sleeping. She liked to sleep late on Sunday. His German shepherd, Max, was right there beside him in the cellar. He opened the window to let the fresh air in and the smoke out. Detective MacDonald sat on his stool and looked at his easel. Painting was his passion in life, especially nature landscapes and the ocean.

With all the violence and evil things he had seen as a detective, this was his way out of that life and into a peaceful scene. Painting to him was like life. He never knew where his paintbrush would take him. With his brush in hand, he started painting on the blank canvas. Today it was the ocean. He started with large strokes of blue and green and shadowed the cloud as if a storm was coming. He knew this was a reflection of his latest discovery, and it was coming through in the painting.

The white sand on the beach was shadowed to add to the mood he was in. Detective MacDonald often went to the beach when he had a case to solve. The sound of the waves and the wind always cleared his head. He sat back on his stool and patted Max as he sat next to him. He lit up a Camel and sat thoughtfully while he smoked.

Now, who, he thought, *would murder the good father in the tub room and be able to move his body to the room unnoticed?* It would have to be someone big and pretty strong to put up with a fight from Father Don. He was at least six feet tall and two-hundred-plus pounds. Also he was a boxer for a time when he was younger, so he could probably hold his own in a fight—unless he was attacked by surprise, which the detective suspected.

From the bloodstains on the wall, Detective MacDonald's first impression was that Father Don's back was facing the perpetrator, and that he was stabbed from behind. He could have even voluntarily entered the tub room to talk to someone privately, but who?

He picked up his brush and added layers of paint to his waves. After an hour, he went upstairs and the dog followed him. He reached down and picked up the Sunday paper from the front porch and settled in the kitchen. Pulling out the *Boston Globe* magazine for Margie and setting it aside, he leafed through the pages and skimmed for a compelling story. He stumbled upon a human-interest story about a priest from Boston transplanted to Yonkers. There was a picture of Father Pat at the Yonkers Treatment Center. The detective widened his eyes. *That home must be cursed*, he thought, shaking his head.

The article revealed that he was now working with teens in recovery. A picture of him with boxing gloves and sparring with the young teens was in the corner of the article.

Apparently Father Pat won the Golden Gloves when he was a young teen himself at the Neighborhood Boxing Club. He was teaching some of the kids how to defend themselves on the street.

Detective MacDonald found this very interesting and coincidental. He had that same thought about Father Don minutes earlier. He put the coffee maker on for another cup of coffee. Margie was up, as the dog was barking in the yard and woke her.

"Oh, I'm sorry, Margie. I was preoccupied with this case and was thinking. I guess I blocked out the barking."

"As you often do, Dave," she said lovingly. She bent down to give a good-morning kiss.

"Sleep well?" she asked.

"Unsettled, you?" he asked.

"Like a log," she said. After working a twelve-hour shift at the hospital, Margie never had trouble sleeping. "Any plans for today? Do you want to take the dog over to Castle Island for a walk?" she asked.

"Sounds great. I just have this one little errand I need to run before we go anywhere. I'll be back soon."

"Shut the screen door on your way out," she yelled.

"See you in a bit," he replied.

He went to his car and headed toward Parkman Street in Dorchester. He parked in front of the gym. It was already open this early.

He walked in the front door and saw there were three practice matches in session.

An older man who looked like he had seen his share of fights approached him.

"Can I help you?" he asked.

Detective MacDonald showed him his badge and asked a few questions. He just wanted to look around, if the owner didn't mind.

"No problem," he said. "Anything I can answer for you?"

Detective MacDonald told him he was looking for someone who boxed there years ago.

"Oh, sure," he said when the detective mentioned Father Pat. "Good boxer. Pat O'Leary, he could have gone pro, he was that good."

The owner guided Detective MacDonald to a wall of pictures with each year and club members framed on the wall. The detective looked at all the pictures and stopped on one in the upper corner of the wall.

"Do you mind if I take this down for a minute to get a closer look?"

The owner took the picture down and handed it to him.

"There's Pat when he was a young teenager."

Detective MacDonald looked closer at the picture and thought he saw a familiar face next to Father Pat.

"Who's this?" he asked.

"Oh, that's Donny O'Sullivan. Those two were always together. Good boxers, the both them."

Detective MacDonald asked if he could make a copy of the picture and then return it.

"No problem. Come back any time, Detective."

He shook his hand and left with the picture. *A coincidence, my ass*, he thought. He got in his car and headed back home.

First thing Monday morning, Detective MacDonald went to visit Matt at the coroner's office. He entered via the back entrance and saw Matt working on an autopsy. He waved to him. Matt gestured to him a full hand, indicating five minutes. MacDonald waited in his office, nursing a cup of coffee. Matt came in soon after.

"How's everything going, Dave?"

"I'd like to reopen the coroner's report on Father Don. I'm wondering about the laceration and the depth of it. I have a feeling that knife was not the murder weapon."

"Why do you think that, Dave?" he asked.

"Well, first of all, new evidence has come forward placing Father Don's murder in the room adjacent to where the body was found. We sprayed the tub room with luminol and there was quite a splatter on the wall. I think he was attacked from behind. The alleged murder weapon would not be able to produce that amount of blood that quickly."

Matt went to his file cabinet and pulled out the findings of the autopsy.

"He had a four-inch laceration on his neck that was deep. He was also on Coumadin, which may have accounted for the rapid blood loss."

"Did you find another weapon?" he asked.

"No, I haven't, but I have a feeling there is one," he said.

"But Father Don's blood was on that weapon," he said.

"That's easy. Whoever did this staged it and put his blood on the Swiss Army knife," the detective explained.

"He did have bruises on his arms as if he was in a struggle and fought back," Matt said. MacDonald got up from his seat.

"Thanks, Matt, that's all I wanted to know.

CHAPTER 25

L ILIAN CONTINUED TO organize Minnie's office and pack up her things. The new director was working out of one of the other offices tempo- rarily. She was reviewing the old VHS tapes that were left over as they replaced the new security system with digital recording.

She went to the cafeteria to get a cup of coffee and a snack and re- turned to her office to view the tapes. She put in the tape she and Minnie had been watching and rewound it for a few minutes. She ate her snack as she watched the tape. *Nothing unusual happening here*, she thought.

No nurses sleeping on the job. As the tape ran, she saw someone walking down the corridor, one of the residents. It appeared that he might have been walking in his sleep or that he couldn't sleep but was wander- ing. He was going from room to room and seemed to putting items in his pocket. The next room he went into, he came out facing the camera. Sure enough, it was Mr. Darcy. Lilian knew he had a problem with insomnia, but she prescribed something for him. *He must have refused his medication*, she thought. He then headed toward the corridor and entered the rectory. Minutes later he came out with more items in his hand and put them in his pocket.

"He's stealing things!" She was aghast.

Lilian continued to watch the tape. She saw Mr. Darcy return to his room with all the paraphernalia he had taken. He was to the nurse's back. She had no clue he was doing this.

Lilian rewound the tape. She wanted to see if there was anything she could recognize in his hand. She saw him return from the visit to the rectory. She put the tape on pause and to her surprise, Mr. Darcy was holding Father Michael's old Swiss Army knife, the one that was supposedly the murder weapon. Lilian couldn't believe it. She couldn't believe that no one told her of his nocturnal behaviors. This, of course, was probably the Alzheimer's dementia.

Sometimes residents would get confused with night and day. She would let Father Michael know about this. He was wondering who was searching through his drawers. *I'll mention this to Steve*, she thought. There needs to be more supervision on the eleven-to-seven shift. While thinking about this, Lilian felt bad she hadn't been able to help him. *If only the nurses reported this, we could have done something. Too late now*, she thought. *I wonder if the family knew.*

What about that knife? That might explain a lot to Detective MacDonald. She would let Father know as soon as possible. In the meantime, she continued to pack up Minnie's things. She would drop them off on her way home from work.

Lilian finished up her day and packed her car with Minnie's things. She just wanted to stop by for a minute. She got on the expressway and took the Cambridge exit. Minnie lived in an apartment complex near Fresh Pond in Cambridge. Lilian parked her car and pressed the buzzer. Minnie came down and let her in. Lilian entered the apartment and noticed a strong smell of marijuana.

"How are you doing?" Lilian asked.

"I'm OK. You know. Now that I'm out of work, I've applied for disability and unemployment at the same time. I'm going to the rehab clinic for the oxy withdrawal."

"Are you supposed to be smoking pot while you're on your meds?" she asked.

"It's OK. I'll be all right," she said.

Lilian dropped off the belongings Minnie had left behind. She didn't want to stay too long, and the smell of the marijuana made her sick to her stomach. She was irritated with Minnie.

"Well, that's all of it," Lilian announced.

"How's the new director working out?" Minnie asked.

"He just started, Minnie. He seems to be doing well. Father Michael seems to like him."

Lilian didn't feel comfortable talking to Minnie too much about work. She said good-bye and headed out to her car. Fortunately she didn't live too far from Minnie's apartment. She would visit another time when Minnie wasn't high. Lilian felt disappointed in Minnie's behavior and just didn't want to deal with her. She hoped the psychiatrist she was seeing would recognize her depression and treat that as well.

Lilian finally made it home. She was early, and the kids were not back from their afternoon sports activities. She decided to take a nap before starting supper.

The next day at work she went to meet with Father Michael. She told him about Mr. Darcy on the tape and that he was night-walking. It was hard to tell whether he was asleep or not.

"I wonder if there are other residents sleepwalking and getting into the rectory," he pondered.

"My drawers have been searched through, but I guess that could be anyone," he said.

She also told him about the Swiss Army knife of his that Mr. Darcy had in his possession, and that it was on the tape. Father Michael was very surprised. That explained how the knife got out of his drawer. He would contact Detective MacDonald in the morning to let him know of this new development. The case had now been reopened. Any information he had, he was sure Detective MacDonald would welcome, especially this new development with the murder weapon.

Father Michael got his jacket and told the front desk to call him on his cell phone if they needed him. He got in his car and drove onto the expressway toward Gloucester. It was early afternoon and the traffic would not pick up till after four. He followed the road to Wingaersheek Beach. He wanted to be near the ocean and out of South Boston. He headed to the beach, parked, and took his shoes off. He started walking along the beach. He lit up a Pall Mall. There were some families on the beach and other walkers just strolling along the shoreline.

The waves were breaking on the boulders that lined part of the beach. The sand was almost white, it was so clean. The wind was blowing in his face, and he just felt calmer and relaxed at the water. He kept walking with his sunglasses on, and then he heard someone calling his name in the distance.

"Father Miiiike," someone was calling. He turned back and he saw a middle-aged woman in a floppy hat and sundress. As she came closer, he recognized who it was.

"Jenn, my goodness, what a small world," he said.

"I live in Gloucester, Father, don't you remember?" she reminded him.

"I do remember, now that you mention it."

"What are you doing this far from home?" she asked

"I'm just took a little drive out of the city. And you, Jenn?"

"I'm here with my daughter. We like to walk the beach in the afternoon," she said. "Come, I'll walk with you. She's back resting over there. Her baby is due soon and we were spending some mother-daughter time together before the new arrival."

Father Michael and Jenn walked at a good clip along Wingaersheek Beach. After they returned, Father Michael bid his good-bye and turned back when Jenn called to him.

"Father, are you headed to the Irish Pub?"

He was surprised. He only thought Father Don knew about the Pub.

"Word gets around, Father, it's a small town. My daughter is headed home and Henry is still at work. I'll go with you," she said. Jenn packed up her things and followed Father Michael to the Irish Pub.

They arrived at the bar, and Father Michael and Jenn ordered their drinks. Father Michael ordered a gin and tonic and Jenn ordered a Corona Light.

"Why don't you get something to eat, Father? You shouldn't be drinking that on an empty stomach."

"Only if you do," he said. Jenn looked at the menu and ordered a turkey club sandwich with a side of sweet potato fries. Father Michael ordered the same.

Father Michael liked Jenn. She was very wholesome, practical, and a good listener. They spent the afternoon talking, and soon it was time to hit the road.

"It was nice to see you, Father. You take care of yourself now. If you come back this way again, make sure you look me up. Henry comes down here a lot. He'll keep you company. You be careful driving home now. I'll see you at work when I return from my vacation."

Father Michael left feeling like a burden had been lifted. He appreciated Jenn's company and would call if he did return. *A lot of memories here*, he thought. Father Don was not too far from his thoughts.

He arrived back at the rectory and the receptionist let him know Detective MacDonald had called a few times. Father Michael was about to call him but looked at the time and decided to let it wait till morning.

He did not want to spoil a perfectly good day.

CHAPTER 26

CRYSTAL WAS VERY busy at work. There was a big trial coming up, and she was preparing papers for her supervising attorney. John and Crystal had become quite an item. Every dinner John attended or conference, there right beside him was Crystal. He even had her freelance for him in assisting with some cases.

John was planning on running for attorney general and felt that Crystal would be the perfect partner in his life, politically and personally.

Crystal was doing very well herself since the brief hospitalization that she had.

John was very cognizant of Crystal's condition; his younger brother had schizophrenia, so John was not unaware of the difficulties in having a mental illness. He thought Crystal was wonderful. She managed things very well, and he wanted to take care of her.

John was not too fond of her brother, Tom. It seemed at every turn, he was trying to control Crystal. John didn't like that. Crystal, having such a trusting nature, seemed to be oblivious to his manipulations. John had recently given notice at the Mansard House. He wanted to start his own law practice or work in a more prestigious law firm in the downtown Boston area. He was thinking about his future, which included Crystal. John didn't care that Crystal had basically become a millionaire.

He truly loved her for herself. Her brother, however, was very concerned with the inheritance and was still waiting for a verdict from the judge regarding the will. Tom really did feel that half of his father's money was his, despite what the will said. He felt entitled to it.

Yes, he knew Crystal might need the money, but she didn't know how to invest that kind of money, and she didn't really care about it. She basically wanted the house. That's what Tom thought. He also thought that her new boyfriend would know what to do with all of that money. Tom was becoming a little jealous now that Crystal seemed to listen to John more than she did to him.

Where is the loyalty? he thought. *We've always been so close, and now he's come between us. Maybe John should take a little vacation, maybe a permanent vacation.* Of course, Crystal would be sad at first, but then she would get over it.

While Tom was daydreaming, he wandered over to the coffee shop across the street from his home in Plymouth. He noticed there was a new waitress working, an attractive woman around his age.

He ordered a cup of coffee and a coffee roll and struck up a conversation with her.

"Are you new in town? I come to this shop all the time, and I've never seen you here," he said.

"Oh, I've just moved to the area. Just starting over, you know, divorce and all. I try to keep busy," she said.

"Tell me about it," he said. "Been there, done that."

This caught her interest since she recently separated from her husband and was vulnerable to any sympathy she could get.

"It's very difficult to be on your own after being married," he said.

She fell right into his sympathies. "It really is, and lonely," she said.

"Do you have any children?" Tom asked.

"I have an older daughter. She's on her own, working full-time, boyfriend. She has her own life." She sighed.

"Well, it was nice talking to you. I'll drop in again. You take care now," he said.

He paid his bill at the counter and left her a sizable tip. She watched him leave, and she thought, *What a nice guy.* Her sensibilities were clouded by his charms.

Crystal was at home cooking dinner for John. She enjoyed cooking tremendously and especially for John. He was always so excited at what she made and was so impressed that she was a chef. She did think about returning to the Culinary Institute to finish what she started. It was getting late, around eight o'clock, and she had just finished making her special sauce for the salmon.

She heard something at the front door and went to open it. As she walked down the hall, someone covered her mouth and pulled her away from the door. Crystal was frantic.

Oh my God, what is this? Whoever it was had a good grip around her throat. She could tell he had a wool stocking cap over his head; she felt it against the side of her face.

Oh my God, she thought, *I think I'm going to faint.* With that thought, Crystal passed out right on the living room floor. The intruder proceeded to take whatever he could carry out the back door. There was a truck waiting near the back kitchen door. He ran upstairs into Mr. Darcy's room and, with the combination, opened up the wall safe and emptied its contents. He heard someone ringing the front doorbell, so he ran downstairs and pulled off his mask. He ran to the back door and closed it, then he walked hurriedly to the front door and opened it to John.

"John, call 911, I just arrived and found Crystal on the floor. She must have fainted," he urged.

John ran to Crystal's side and felt for her pulse. He immediately called 911 and kept calling Crystal's name to rouse her.

"What happened?" he yelled.

"I don't really know," Tom said. I was just passing by to check up on Crystal and found her like this. She's on those strong medications; maybe she had a bad reaction."

The sound of the siren was heard in the distance. John kept calling Crystal and she started to come to. She saw John over her and Tom beside him.

Crystal started screaming, "Someone attacked me. He choked me." Her screaming turned to crying. The ambulance arrived and paramedics were on the scene. John tried to calm her down, but to no avail. The paramedics led her out to the ambulance and John went with her.

"I'll stay here and lock up," Tom stated.

"That's a good idea, Tom. Call the police and report the incident. I'll stay with Crystal."

Tom closed the door and waited till the ambulance was out of sight. He continued to take what he could out to the van. He would call the police in a while and report the intruder, but not now.

He went into the kitchen and saw the delicious meal Crystal was preparing for John and was suddenly hungry. He sat down at the table and took his time helping himself to salmon, rice, and the special sauce. He had no shame in what he was doing and felt he was not doing anything wrong. After all, it was his parents' house. He finished his meal and washed it down with the merlot that was already poured into the wine glasses. Tom left through the front door and locked it. He walked around the back and even waved to the neighbors as he rode away in his white van. He never called the police to report the break-in. He would tell John, in all the excitement and concern for Crystal's well-being, he forgot.

CHAPTER 27

DETECTIVE MACDONALD CALLED Father Michael regarding the latest information on the case. He informed him of the findings in the tub room. Father Michael informed him of Mr. Darcy's roaming at night and his wandering into the rectory as well as stealing his Swiss Army knife. Detective MacDonald did not tell Father of his suspicions. He thanked him for the information and said he would be in touch. In the meantime Detective MacDonald was getting ready to take a long drive to Yonkers, New York. Officer Ed was taking the trip with him. He was making a surprise visit to see Father Pat. The fact that Father Pat and Father Don were boxers together in their younger days was a mystery to him. Why didn't Father Pat mention this to him when he interviewed him? He felt that omission was just as bad as lying. MacDonald and Ed started out their journey by stopping at the donut shop first.

They ordered two coffees, one regular and one black. Detective MacDonald also ordered two plain crullers for the long ride. They headed onto I- 93 north from Neponset Circle, headed west onto Route 90, the Massachusetts Turnpike. The ride took them five hours. Once in Yonkers, they headed toward the outskirts following the route on the GPS.

The place was beautiful. It looked like a country club to the detectives. They parked their car in the visitor's lot and proceeded to the front office.

"We are here to visit with Father Pat O'Leary," MacDonald said.

"He may be in a group session. Is he expecting you?" the receptionist asked.

"No, we are here on official police business," he said. He showed her his detective badge.

The receptionist picked up the phone and called the floor.

"He'll be down in five minutes. Gentlemen, you can wait over there in the waiting area," she said.

Five minutes later Father Pat was greeting Detective MacDonald.

"How are you, Detective? What brings you all the way to Yonkers?" he asked.

"I came to see you, Father, to ask you a few questions."

He was direct and came to the point of his visit.

"I understand that Father Don and you were boxers when you were young and that you both were in the Neighborhood Boxing Club. Is that true?" he asked.

"Yes it is, and what about it?" Father Pat answered.

"We uncovered new information regarding Father Don's murder. Where were you on that morning of the murder, Father Pat?"

"Haven't we been through this, Detective?"'

"Just answer the question please."

"I was on Mansard six passing out medications to the residents. My shift started at 7:00 a.m."

"Which would give you time to go down two flights and into the tub room to murder Father Don," Detective MacDonald said. "His time of death was estimated at six a.m., Father. That gave you time to leave the rectory, meet Father Don in the hallway, persuade him to go into the tub room, and attack him from behind."

"I don't believe this, you're making things up!" he cried.

"That's the way I see it, Father. You were both boxers. You were blackmailing him by threatening to disclose his relationship with Ziggy and revealing that he had a child. Also you were trying to extort money from him. You're a boxer, he was a boxer. You are about the same height and weight. You look pretty strong to me. You attacked him from behind and stabbed him with a thin-bladed knife. The alleged murder weapon in Mr. Darcy's room was placed there on purpose for someone to find. You then dragged the body and arranged it on the floor and let him continue to bleed. You then washed your hands and went back to Mansard six and continued with your med pass."

"Wow! That's quite a story, but I think you're wrong. You forgot one thing, Detective: I have an alibi. I was in the chapel with the other priests the whole time. We say our morning prayers daily from six o'clock to seven. As a matter of fact I was standing next to Father Michael. Your story is a good one, but I'm afraid you're mistaken. Unless you have a warrant for my arrest, I'm going to go back to my room."

He then left and walked up the stairwell back to his room.

"He has you there, Dave, we don't have a warrant and you know this is all speculation," Ed chimed in.

"Of course, I know that. I'm just letting him simmer. He might crack and confess later. Let's go home."

They both left and headed toward the parking lot. Detective MacDonald's stomach was grumbling. His ulcer was acting up.

"Why don't we go over to that restaurant? It looks pretty good," MacDonald said.

"Isn't that a vegetarian place? I hate those places, I can never get anything good to eat."

"You might be surprised. Margie is a vegetarian, and we often go out to eat in vegetarian restaurants. The food is actually pretty good."

"Whatever you say. You're the boss."

After their meal Detective MacDonald and Officer Ed headed home to Boston. The weather was getting cloudy and rain was in the forecast. It was a long way to drive in the rain. They hadn't stayed more than two hours on their visit, and they left around five o'clock in the evening. MacDonald let Ed drive since he drove up and was tired. Detective MacDonald leaned back on the headrest. Ed programmed the GPS to guide them home to Boston.

Detective MacDonald closed his eyes and tried to sort out the facts in his head. He was thinking about Father Pat's story and had to admit it had a ring of truth to it. Also he didn't seem like he was lying. He looked him right in the eye and gave a plausible answer to everything. He knew Ziggy was not the killer, ruled out Father Michael, who was still in mourning, but he still had his suspicions about Tom, Mr. Darcy's son. He would visit him next, even though he found the whole experience with him unpleasant. That one had a temper. He still needed to interview Minnie.

He fell asleep, and when he woke up, they were entering Connecticut.

"I can take over the driving, Ed," he said.

"Naw, I'm OK. I don't mind driving. It relaxes me," he said.

MacDonald called into the station to check with the officer on duty for the night shift. The officer informed him of the attack on Crystal Darcy and said she was being treated in the hospital. John McDevitt called it in. Detective MacDonald was very surprised. What was that about? *Well*, he thought, *Crystal is a multimillionaire now. Maybe she should get a security system installed.*

Pretty soon they were crossing into Massachusetts. They made it back to the station at midnight. Detective MacDonald checked all his messages and then headed home for the night.

There was a message from John McDevitt. It sounded urgent, but MacDonald needed to get home because Margie was waiting up for him. He would call Mr. McDevitt in the morning.

The next morning he returned John's call. Apparently the attacker also stole some of Crystal's belongings in the house, valuable ones. He would send Ed over to further investigate. He had a suspicion of who might have done this. In the meantime, John was very upset about this and vowed he would not leave Crystal alone ever again. With her permission, he had the locks changed and set up an advanced security system. John was going to move in with Crystal as well. He knew her brother would disapprove, but maybe not after what happened to his sister. Detective MacDonald also called Father Michael to tell him about his visit with Father Pat.

Father Michael knew all about it. He really didn't think Father Pat had anything to do with Father Don's murder. *But who knows. I'm not a detective*, he thought. His main concern right now was the financial situation of the Home. With Father Paul's assistance, a lot of wasteful spending was being managed and the census was up.

He was happy about that. Also, he was waiting to hear about the property across the street from the L Street bathhouse. It was a three-family house for sale and would be perfect for an assisted living facility for the elderly. The income would not hurt and keep both places viable.

Father Michael saw Jenn that morning as she returned from her vacation.

"Has the state come thru yet, Father?" she asked.

"Not yet," he said.

"Any day, no surprises here, we all know the drill."

Jenn left and proceeded with her routine for the day. She did not mention her encounter with Father Michael at the beach, as she did not want to remind him. She knew he was grieving Father Don's death and was having a hard time. She wanted Father to meet up with Henry, who ran a local chapter of AA near the Irish Pub and was friends with the owner.

The owner, Joe, had a drinking problem, and Henry was his sponsor. Jenn thought it might help Father if he had someone to talk to. He was drinking a lot.

CHAPTER 28

TOM WENT TO visit with Crystal in the hospital. He acted as if he was very concerned for her welfare. John did not have any idea that Tom was involved in the assault on Crystal. He was too close to the situation to see him for what he was, a narcissist.

In fact, Tom had all the traits of a narcissistic personality disorder.

He really had no empathy for Crystal and was mostly concerned with himself and his needs. John knew he didn't like him, but he made an effort to be civil because Tom was Crystal's brother.

"Hi, Crystal, how are you feeling? What an ordeal this has been for you," he said.

"I'm OK now, Tom. John is going to stay with me for a while, and we're installing a security system first thing in the morning. The workmen will be there at ten tomorrow morning. John will let them in. I want it set up before I set foot in that house again."

Well, Tom thought, *so that was that. My days of pilfering are over.* No matter, he had all he needed from his father's estate and was in the process of auctioning it off. He set up an overseas account to avoid paying taxes on the items. He already had over $400,000 in his account. The next step was to wait for the verdict on the will. Would it be in his favor? Only time would tell.

Tom had a buyer for the painting that he stole from the house. He knew that would make him financially secure for the rest of his life. Crystal still had no idea that the original was not in the frame.

"Oh Tom, by the way, the appraiser will be coming by the end of the week. I thought you might like to know," she said. Tom braced himself when she said that, and John noticed he acted a little strange with that news.

"Crystal, will you be giving me a new set of keys for the house?" he asked before he left.

"I don't think so, not this time," she said. "John will be living with me so it will be our place. If you want to come by, just call me."

Tom bristled at the sound of that. He said good-byes and headed for home.

On the way back to Plymouth, he stopped at the coffee shop and ordered a coffee regular (with cream and sugar) and a corn muffin. The waitress that he met last time was on duty.

"Well, hello, stranger, how are you doing today?" she said. "I can't recall your name."

"It's Tom, and yours is?" he said.

"Terry," she said.

"It's nice to see you again. I know this might sound forward, but would you like to get a bite to eat sometime?" he offered.

"Sure, that sounds swell. I usually get off from work about nine." She was excited.

"How about this Friday? I know a nice steakhouse right on the out-skirts of Plymouth."

"That's great. Can you pick me up here?" she said.

"I think it might be easier if I meet you there," he said.

Tom gave her the name of the steakhouse and waved good-bye on the way out.

His wife's friend Monica was right in the corner of the shop. She was reading the paper, so Tom did not see her. She saw everything that transpired. She couldn't believe Tom.

What a sleaze, she thought. *I'm not going to tell Claire, not just yet. Let's see how this plays out. It looks like he's up to his old tricks.* She didn't want to be the one to tell her, after she seemed so happy last time she saw her.

Minutes later Tom was home. Claire had prepared a delicious dinner for them both.

"Tom, dinner's ready whenever you are. I made your favorite meal, salmon with that special sauce Crystal makes. She gave me the recipe. How is Crystal doing anyway? Did you get a chance to visit with her in the hospital?" Claire inquired.

Tom sat down to dinner with Claire and relayed the whole situation with Crystal and John. Claire was happy for them. *John seemed so caring and concerned for her well-being, unlike Tom,* she thought.

"That's lovely. She needs someone. I'm genuinely happy for her," she said.

"Oh really?" Tom screamed at Claire. "You know what this means, don't you? If they get married, John will get everything she owns, being her spouse."

He slammed the chair against the table and walked away into the den. Claire was stunned. *What is wrong with him? If he thinks I'm putting up with this nightmare, he's crazy.*

She removed herself from the dining room and grabbed her pocketbook and phone. She slammed the door on the way out. She called her friend Monica to see if she wanted to catch a movie.

CHAPTER 29

ZIGGY MET WITH Daniel the next day. They both decided they wanted to see more of each other. She confided in Daniel regarding her son Sami and her relationship with Father Don.

Daniel understood. He knew she needed space and knew that the relationship would not go too far while Ziggy was in mourning. They decided to start running and training for the Boston Marathon. This would be a good time to do it since the marathon was not until April.

In the meantime Ziggy worked hard at her job as a nursing assistant and was starting nursing school in September. Things were really moving along for her. *At least*, she thought, *I have hope for the future.*

Elisabeth was working in the kitchen at the nursing home in Chelsea. She was a senior this year and was planning on attending college in the fall. Elisabeth got accepted to Charlestown Community College,. She was becoming accustomed to life in America, especially the freedom she had and the ability to make her own decisions. She enjoyed having her own money and found working very rewarding. Some of her other friends that she met at school were talking about getting an apartment together, but the time was not right for her. Ziggy needed help with the finances and Elisabeth was willing to help her with the expenses. Daniel was almost finished with his pharmacy training. He received a job at a local pharmacy in Chelsea and would be starting soon.

Ziggy decided to call Father Michael to see how he was feeling. She knew he took Father Don's death very hard, as she did. It has been five months now since the murder. She knew it was going to take a long time for her. The six-month anniversary Mass was coming up soon. Ziggy decided it was OK to talk to him now that some time had passed. She was sitting at the kitchen counter and decided to call today. She dialed his number and the phone started ringing. Christina, the housemaid answered.

"Father Michael, please," she asked. Soon he was on the receiver.

"Hello, Father Michael, it's Ziggy. I'm just calling to say hello and to see how you are doing," she said.

"Just fine, Ziggy, how are you? Are you working now?" he asked.

Ziggy told him about everything that was happening in her life as well as her acceptance to UMass Boston. They talked for a while, and finally Father Michael told her to come and visit while she was at school in the fall, as the Mansard House was close to the university.

"Please bring little Sami for a visit as well," he said. She wished him well and said good-bye. She would be there at St George's in October for the six-month memorial Mass. In the meantime her siblings were thriving in school and becoming more familiar with their new home in America.

Ziggy was happy that Daniel lived nearby and would spend some time with her and her family. Daniel would come by on Sundays for dinner and they would sit and chat for hours and drink espresso. She would make Ethiopian bread on Sunday to go with their meal. She had started to attend the Coptic Church in Boston on Sunday. Daniel happily attended, too, and afterward they would socialize with the other families. Slowly her grief was in the background of her life and was being replaced with happiness and a sense of belonging. Daniel visited often, and they were thinking of renting a big house in Chelsea where both families could live together. Having some men in the house appealed to Ziggy.

Since her parents' death, she worried about her younger brother and felt Daniel would be the perfect role model for him. Also it would benefit Sami. Father Michael understood Ziggy's desire to separate from any life having to do with her past. He understood her struggles and her grief. She had a lot to deal with from the past and she did very well. However, grief has a way of catching up with you through different avenues. Father Michael chose a strong drink every now and then; Ziggy chose to block it from her mind and to isolate herself from people who knew Father Don. Both ways eased the pain.

Detective MacDonald was putting all the pieces together. Father Don's murder investigation was ongoing. First the original weapon had been removed as evidence. But he had yet to find the real murder weapon. It appeared to him the whole crime scene was a setup since the victim was dragged from the tub room nearby to Mr. Darcy's room. The motive for the murder had to be anger, jealousy, or greed. Or was it something else?

The visit to Yonkers proved only one thing: that Father Pat had an alibi and he and the victim were old friends, even though he was blackmailing him. Of course Father Pat explained that away, that he was desperate and his own life was being threatened from a gambling debt.

The trail of the three priests proved they were actually loan sharks collecting a debt that Father Pat owed. They were never found.

The only two suspects left to investigate further were Minnie, now unemployed, and Tom, Crystal's brother. Both were in the home at the time of the murder. Minnie was covering for an evening supervisor who had called in sick earlier that day. Tom was visiting with his father early that morning.

Mr. Darcy apparently was a night owl and was stealing items from everyone's rooms, including Father Michael. The tapes showed he was the one who took the Swiss Army knife from the rectory. It obviously was in his possession and someone knew about it.

Detective MacDonald decided to give Minnie a visit to question her about that morning. Maybe she could shed some light on anything suspicious going on. Before that, he would interview the night nurse to see why she had been out that evening.

Father Michael and Ziggy were obviously cleared and were still grieving. The revelation that Ziggy's baby was Father Don's child was a stunner but made sense to him. Things happen. *What are you going to do?* He thought.

Detective MacDonald sent his Officer Ed to interview the night nurse. Back at the station, he called Minnie to set up a time to visit with her. He had found out about her illness and drug addiction to painkillers from Father Michael. He was sorry to hear that she had that problem. A lot of people did.

He knew Minnie wasn't fond of him and that the visit might get prickly, but it was necessary. He arrived at her apartment in Fresh Pond and parked his car on the street. He walked to the apartment complex and rang the bell for her apartment. Her roommate answered. She had just returned from work. She worked as a physical therapist at Mercy Hospital in Cambridge. She helped Minnie a lot with her exercises for her Parkinson's.

"Hello, I'm here to see Minnie McCracken," he said.

"Sure. Come right on in. I'll let her know you are here. You can wait in the living room."

Her roommate left. Five minutes later, Minnie came into the room.

"How are you, Detective? I didn't expect to see you again," she said.

"I know that, but some new developments have come forward, and I just had a few questions."

"Go ahead," she replied.

"Why were you covering that shift on the day of Father Don's murder?" he asked

"My night nurse's daughter was sick. Because it was last minute, there was no one to cover, so I had to do it," she said

"Were you there at six in the morning?"

"Yes, I was the only one passing out meds. The other night nurse was down on her break."

"Did you see or hear anything suspicious? Was anyone visiting with Mr. Darcy?"

"Well, his son, Tom, usually comes in around that time to visit, but I didn't see him that morning," she stated.

"What about Father Don? Did you see him?"

"I did see him. He was visiting and passing out Communion to the residents that were awake."

"What time was that?"

"Around five in the morning."

"Well, the time of death was estimated to be at six o'clock. Did you hear anything?" he asked.

"No, nothing," she said, "but I was at the opposite end of the unit. The floor curves around to the other side, so anyone could have come and gone and I wouldn't have seen them."

"Did you leave the floor for any reason?" he asked.

"I did," she said. "I left to take a fifteen-minute break when the other nurse came back. I didn't see or hear anything suspicious."

"OK, well, thank you for your cooperation, Minnie. I'll be in touch if I have any more questions," he said.

"I'm sure you will, Detective."

She then led him to the front door and bid him a good day. He left but wasn't sure if he bought her story.

CHAPTER 30

TOM LEFT HOME around 5:30 p.m. Claire was out with her friends. Tom was looking forward to Friday night to meet with Terry. He was going to a steakhouse in Kingston. It was far enough away from Plymouth so he thought it was safe enough to go without being noticed. He arrived at 7:00 p.m. and saw Terry waiting inside. He promptly walked over to the table.

"I'm sorry," he said. "I'm a little late. The traffic was bad."

"That's OK, no worries," she said.

Terry was happy to have some company for dinner. They ordered their meal and decided to have some wine first. Terry was very talkative and told Tom the whole story about her divorce and her feelings, something he really didn't want to hear. He basically wanted a night out to relax, and so far it wasn't going the way he wanted. He was sympathetic to her story but chose not to reveal too much about his past.

They completed their dinner and moved on to a small cozy bar on the outskirts of Plymouth. Terry could hold her liquor, and Tom had a feeling that she'd been drinking for a while. *It's one way to drown your sorrows*, he thought.

In the meantime Claire was out with her friend Monica. They decided to try a paint bar, the latest craze combining a painting lesson with drinks. She was having a great time until Monica had a little too much to drink and began to tell Claire about her recent observation at the coffee shop in her neighborhood in Plymouth.

Claire was so upset that she suddenly felt like someone had punched her in the stomach. Monica proceeded to tell Claire all of the details of Tom's recent fling. Claire was devastated.

"He's such a jerk, Claire. I don't know how you put up with him" Monica said.

"I should have guessed. All the signs were there, the new clothes, recent haircut, new cologne. How could I be so blind?" Claire started to cry.

"I'm so sorry to break the news to you, Claire. I just thought you needed to know". Monica said apologetically. "If it was me, I would want to know." She said.

Claire was so sick of Tom and his cheating ways. It wasn't the first time. She thought, *Once a cheater, always a cheater*. She thought about the story he gave her about love and forgiveness. What a crock! Claire suddenly decided to go home. She felt sick. Monica had too much to drink, so she dropped her off first. Claire entered the house and poured a glass of wine for herself. She decided to wait up for Tom and see what excuse he was going to give her now.

Walking down to the basement, she removed the key from her pants pocket. She hoped it would open the wooden chest that Tom had hidden there. She opened it up. *Oh my goodness*, she thought, *he's such a thief and a liar*. He'd stolen most of Mr. and Mrs. Darcy's jewelry collection as well as her irreplaceable silver coffee service... Rummaging through, she could see there were various pieces of sculpture and artwork. While she was searching, she came upon a wool cap with a face mask on it.

Oh my God! she thought. *What did Tom do?* Suddenly she was afraid for herself. She knew the person who broke into Crystal's house was wearing a wool face mask. Tom was there the whole time pretending to be sympathetic and explaining that he just dropped by.

Claire ran upstairs. She called the police and explained her concern and fear. Ten minutes later a patrol car was at her house. After what Claire told him, the officer called Detective MacDonald. The detective arrived fifteen minutes later.

He searched the basement and the contents of the chest. Claire said she did not know that all of this jewelry was here. The face mask is what interested Detective MacDonald.

The contents of the stolen goods had been reported missing by Crystal Darcy after the break-in. Crystal had no idea that Tom was the one stealing her belongings.

Finally, around 10:30 p.m., Tom came strolling in. He saw the police cars out front and thought that something happened to Claire. Tom looked at the scene in front of him. The police approached him and handcuffed him.

"What the hell is going on here?" he screamed.

"Mr. Tom Darcy, you are under arrest for the attempted murder of your sister, Crystal Darcy. You are also being charged with breaking-and-entering and grand larceny."

The police officer then read him his Miranda rights. Tom left screaming and yelling.

"Claire, call my attorney. I want you to make bail tonight," he yelled at her.

Claire looked at him square in the face and said,

"Go to hell, Tom. Call the attorney yourself."

She slammed the door and watched the patrol car drive away. She would go to court the next morning to file for a divorce and a restraining order. She went back into the living room and poured herself another glass of wine.

The next morning Crystal received the news from Claire that Tom was arrested. She called the precinct and spoke to Detective MacDonald. She couldn't believe it, her own brother.

Taking the material items was not what bothered her so much, but the fact he strangled her till she fainted. John couldn't believe the lengths to which Tom would go to disgrace himself. He just was no good; Crystal had to face that fact.

"I don't want you ever to be alone in the same room with him again, " he said. "He's a psychopath."

Crystal knew Tom had problems. She was just so upset that he tried to hurt her. She didn't think he would go that far for material possessions. Suddenly she was very sad and started to cry.

"Crystal, it's OK," John said. "This has been a huge shock for you, calm down now. Please don't take it so hard. I don't want you to get sick."

He held her in his arms till she calmed down.

"You know, John, I'm so lucky I have you in my life. What would I have done if I had to handle this alone? You have been so supportive," she said. "I really love you, John." She smiled.

"Crystal, I love you with all my heart. I'm never going to leave you alone again."

They stood in the living room of Crystal's house with their arms around each other, embracing.

* * *

The next morning Crystal called the attorney who was handling her father's will.

"I want to stop the appeal," she said. "I don't agree anymore to the contestation of the will and want it stopped," she said. Her attorney would contact the judge and have the will placed back into its original context. Crystal had no intention of having anything else taken away from her. The contents of the will would remain the same, including the money left to the Mansard House and the priest's retirement fund. She didn't know if she could ever face Tom again.

Detective MacDonald received a search warrant for Tom's house. He collected and catalogued all the items Tom had stolen from his father's house and submitted them as evidence against him.

Tom was booked on charges and held in jail till the hearing. The judge refused home arrest secondary to the nature of the crime and flight risk. Actually Tom had nowhere to go since Claire got a restraining order and filed for a divorce that same day.

CHAPTER 31

LILIAN DECIDED TO go visit Minnie after her shift was over. She drove over to her apartment and slowly got out of her car. She didn't know what condition Minnie would be in.

Lilian rang the bell and Minnie answered. She seemed OK and Lilian entered her apartment.

They sat in the kitchen. Minnie made some coffee and they had muffins Lilian had brought with her. She made them fresh that morning. The muffins were delicious. Lilian gave her an update of what was going on at work. The new director was working out well, and Father Paul was now an assistant administrator.

Minnie seemed depressed to Lilian. She asked about her latest visit to the psychiatrist and what meds she was now taking. The treatment program for the oxycodone withdrawal was hard for her. She didn't like talking in support groups, and she thought the social worker who was their group leader didn't know how to handle everyone's problems. Lilian felt that Minnie just didn't want to go and was still in denial about her problem.

"Detective MacDonald came snooping around," Minnie said.

"What is his problem? Does he think everyone had something to do with Father Don's murder?

"He's so annoying with all his questions."

"What was he asking you?" Lilian asked.

"He wanted to know if Tom Darcy was there in the morning and why I was covering that morning."

Lilian was surprised.

"Oh, I didn't know you were in that early," Lilian said.

"I was covering for Mary, the night nurse, because her daughter was sick," Minnie replied.

"Did you see Father Don on the floor while you were there?" she asked.

"I did see him around five o'clock. He was giving Communion to the residents."

"Including Mr. Darcy?"

"Yes."

Lilian suddenly got a funny feeling in her stomach. She didn't like what she was thinking.

"Did you know Father Don, Minnie?" she asked.

"What, are you interrogating me as well? I talked to him a few times, what about it?" Minnie said impatiently. Lilian could see that she was getting agitated and decided to leave.

"Oh Minnie, it's running late. I've got to pick up my daughter from school."

She left quickly and saw that Minnie was looking at her suspiciously.

"I'll call you later," she said.

She rushed to her car and left in a hurry. Minnie went back into her bathroom and opened up a small silver pillbox. She took out two oxycodone pills. *I have my own suppliers now,* she thought.

I don't need any nosy priest around asking me questions about medications, or threatening to go to Father Michael with what he knew. Minnie went into the exercise room that her roommate set up for her. She started her usual weight-lifting routine. She was pretty strong now.

Detective MacDonald was reviewing the details of his visit with Minnie. The information from his officer revealed she had a serious drug problem, which no one seemed to talk about. Through sources at the hospital, Detective MacDonald found out that her hospitalization was from a drug overdose, specifically oxycodone—or as the kids call it, cotton. Now she was in a rehabilitation program outpatient. Detective MacDonald knew that it would be difficult for her. The crime scene sweep, especially in the tub room, revealed there were a few pills found on the floor near the scene of the crime. Maybe it was nothing, but maybe it was something.

The lab would tell him soon. He knew a lot of the elderly were on oxy for pain control. How did Minnie get her supply?

A visit to Father Michael is in order, he thought. *He's not telling me everything. Maybe we'll go for a little drive together and get a drink.* That afternoon, Detective MacDonald contacted Father Michael. He wondered if he would like to get together for lunch to review the case. He knew the perfect place. At one o'clock the next day, he picked him up in front of the rectory. Detective MacDonald had an old Crown Vic that needed some repairs, but the engine was good. He took the expressway north and headed for Route 1.

Father Michael turned to him. "Where are we headed, Dave?" he asked.

"Oh, I know this little Irish bar in Gloucester that serves good fish and chips. I thought we could go there. It would give us time to talk on the way."

At this point in the investigation, Father Michael was willing to share everything he knew to uncover who murdered his dear friend.

They arrived at the bar in Gloucester and Father Michael looked at Detective MacDonald and said, "How coincidental. This is the place Father Don and I would escape to from the city, and also to have a drink or two."

"It's not a coincidence, Father," he said. "We had you under surveillance in the initial investigation. We followed you out here. I've been coming myself ever since. It's a great place, great corned beef and cabbage."

Father Michael let out a laugh and smiled. He liked Detective MacDonald and just thought it was funny.

They went inside and ordered their lunch, and both had a Guinness. Father Michael revealed Minnie's situation and her Parkinson's illness. He told him of her erratic and paranoid behavior, probably related to the oxycodone addiction.

The fact that Minnie would risk her livelihood meant she was pretty much hooked.

They both hoped the rehab was working. They finished up their meal and made it back to Boston before the rush-hour traffic. Detective MacDonald gave him his business card again and told Father Michael to call if there were any new developments. Detective MacDonald returned to the precinct. Officer Ed was waiting for him.

"Some new information had been uncovered. Father Don was an addictions counselor in his parish. He was a licensed social worker as well as a priest and used his skills to help in the community. He went back to school at Suffolk University while he was the pastor at St George's Parish. Also, he himself had a drug problem in the past when he was young but beat it."

Detective MacDonald shared the information that there were pills found on the floor near the tub at the crime scene. Soon thereafter the lab report came through the fax. The report stated the pills were Roxicodone—generic name, oxycodone.

CHAPTER 32

CRYSTAL WAS PREPARING the house for John's arrival. She cleaned out the spare bedroom for his desk and home office.

She was depressed at what her brother had done to her. She knew he had a short fuse, but the extent of his selfishness and attempt on her life was unforgivable. Crystal had to let her feelings and anger toward him go and start a whole new life for herself that did not include Tom Darcy. *Not at this point in time anyway*, she thought.

The items Tom stole were returned to her. Some of her mother's jewelry was irreplaceable, and she was very happy to have it back. The paintings were returned as well; she had no idea those were stolen till the appraiser informed her of it.

Even though Crystal was very wealthy now, she wanted to remain at her father's home and continued to work as a paralegal but cut her hours to part-time. She enrolled in the Boston Culinary School and planned on returning in the fall. She needed to keep herself busy, and John encouraged her to return to cooking. Of course there were selfish reasons on his part, but Crystal enjoyed preparing meals for him and delighted in his attentions.

"This is marvelous, Crystal. How did you make this?" he would say.

She would never let him in on her secret ingredients.

"That's under lock and key. No one gets those recipes, trade secrets," she would say. Crystal was wondering how Claire was doing. She must be devastated that Tom was cheating on her. She wondered if Claire knew Tom was stealing things from her. Hopefully she didn't, because if she did it would mean she was an accessory to the crime and that she had no feelings toward Crystal, either. She wouldn't contact her again.

John had left his position at the Mansard House, but he still kept in touch with Father Michael. He was shocked to hear of Minnie McCracken stealing the narcotics at work.

Father Michael told him the new keyboard technology proved that Minnie was stealing the patients' oxycodone for herself. John advised Father Michael to press charges and report her to the board of nursing for ethical misconduct. Not only was she stealing from the patients, but she was putting their health in jeopardy. Father Michael knew he had to do this. He just didn't want to. He felt Minnie's actions were a result of her addiction and her depression from the Parkinson's. In his position he had to report her.

John was correct. It was the right thing to do. He would file the papers in the morning. With a good attorney, she might be spared jail time, but maybe not. For now she was in rehab and would need to stay there. Next week they would start blood tests weekly to make sure she was clean. *There's a price to pay for your actions*, Father Michael thought. Despite everything she did, Father Michael still had compassion for her. He kept Minnie in his daily prayers.

John was happy with his new position as assistant district attorney for the state of Massachusetts. He felt he could make some real changes in the laws, especially in the area of domestic abuse. He was planning on asking Crystal to be his wife. He already picked out the engagement ring.

He had waited this long to find the woman of his dreams, and she was it.

He was turning forty and was eager to start a family. John arrived at Crystal's house at 10:00 a.m. on Sunday morning. The moving van was there before him. Crystal had been up for a few hours and had already made eggs Benedict and homemade hash for John. As he entered the house, he could smell the aroma from the living room.

"Hi, John, come in the kitchen, breakfast is ready. I bought this new espresso coffee machine, and I want to try it out with you."

"Sure," he said. "You know I love strong coffee."

They sat in the kitchen enjoying their breakfast. John had never felt so peaceful in his life. Crystal was fussing with a fruit tart that she made as John put his arms around her.

"You know, Crystal, this is a big step for us. What do you think if we make it permanent? We're too old to be moving in together like young kids. What do you think? Will you marry me, Crystal?"

With that, he pulled out a jewelry box with a one-carat diamond ring. It was simple and feminine, just like Crystal. She loved it.

"Yes, that's my answer. I thought you'd never ask! We are going to be so happy together," she said.

"Crystal McDevitt," he said. "That sounds right to me. Crystal, I love you with all my heart. I never thought my life would change like this or that I would ever find someone like you." Crystal felt the same.

They finished up their breakfast, and then the doorbell rang. The movers were ready to start moving in John's furniture. Behind them, Crystal saw Claire coming up the steps. She stopped at the front door and waited for Claire to say something.

"Crystal, I just wanted to come by and say how sorry I was for everything Tom put you through," she said. "I did know he was stealing things from the house, but you know Tom, he thought he was entitled to everything. I never brought it up to him. Frankly I didn't know what to do. Then, when I saw the mask, I knew it had gone beyond taking things from his father's house."

"If you knew, Claire, you could have done something earlier, so it didn't have to turn to violence," Crystal said. She knew the real reason Claire called the police was that she had the goods on Tom, and he was cheating on her.

"I just wanted to let you know how I felt. In hindsight, yeah, I should have called the police earlier."

"Just so you know, Claire, my father's will is not being contested. He was of sound mind at the time he wrote it. It's remaining as written the day it was read to Tom. Please don't come by here again. We are not family. You just happen to be married to my brother. We are not blood."

She closed the door in Claire's face before she could say another word.

CHAPTER 33

FATHER MICHAEL SAT at the bank, passing papers on the house that the corporation bought to set up an assisted living program. The house was across the street from the L Street bathhouse and allowed a perfect view from the porch to the beach. There would need to be some renovations, of course, but Father Michael expected that. The next day he was back at the facility doing his usual morning walk-through.

The facility was due for its state inspection any day now that the window for inspection was closing. It was a chilly morning as Father Michael walked past the time clock. He could feel the first hint of fall approaching in late August. *The summer sure flew by fast*, he thought. *It's almost September.*

He saw a group of five ladies with briefcases and notebooks in hand enter the building. The state inspectors had arrived.

The announcement was made and flyers were posted, announcing the surveyors were in the building. The survey would last a maximum of five days. The survey team set up camp in one of the main conference rooms. Day one started without a hitch. On days two and three, their investigation and observation were in full force. Kitchens and store rooms were inspected. Nurses were monitored for medication pass. Charts were reviewed for accuracy of documentation, and finally residents were interviewed for any concerns and questions. On day four, the maintenance walk-through, the inspector went up to the roof deck to check the wiring. In her inspection, she noted the beautiful display of colored pots and flowering plants. She went over to admire them and spotted the decorated handle of a garden trowel in one of the pots.

"Isn't that pretty?" she said. "Look at the detail in the handle of that garden trowel."

She pulled out the trowel from the pot and was surprised that it was a knife and not a trowel.

"Well, what do we have here?" she said. "This is so unusual. Is this supposed to be here?" she asked the maintenance director.

He took the knife and looked at it closely. It appeared there were some dried bloodstains on it. The decorated handle had an inscription on it, "Antigonish, Nova Scotia." It was a spring-assisted knife that closed up into the holder. The maintenance director folded it in place and held it in his hand.

The surveyor continued her inspection and found no deficiencies as she headed back down the elevator to the main floor. The maintenance director paged Father Michael and met him in his office.

"I'm not sure whose this is," he said, and handed the knife over to Father Michael.

"It's a spring-assisted model. See the button? You touch it and the blade pops out," he said.

"Thank you, I'll take care of it. Maybe someone left it while they were repotting some of the plants," Father Michael said. He knew that wasn't what it was used for, but he had nothing else to say.

The next day the state exited, as they found no violations. Father Michael called Detective MacDonald with the news that another knife was found on the roof deck. The detective arrived fifteen minutes later and placed the knife into an evidence bag and sent it off to forensics.

He then went up to the roof with the maintenance man to investigate where the knife was found. He took the pot back to the crime lab to have the soil analyzed.

Detective MacDonald headed home for a nice dinner Margie had prepared for him. It was her night off from work, and they always had dinner together when she was off.

She made his favorite meatloaf, mashed potatoes, and corn. His mouth watered when he thought about it. He arrived home about six, and Margie met him at the front door.

"How was your day, hon?" she asked.

"The usual," he answered back. He didn't like bringing work home and never talked about his cases. Margie knew he was always thinking;

she didn't want to pry and also wanted to give him a break from the pressures of his job.

He gave her a big hug and a kiss. He went upstairs to change into his worn-out jeans and T-shirt. He liked to be really comfortable when he was home. Max was already jumping around waiting for a walk.

"OK, boy, settle down. I need to have my dinner and unwind first. Then we will go for a walk."

Max knew the signals from the tone in his voice. He sat down by the stove and waited patiently for dinner to be finished. The two of them took their coffee out to the back porch to have a smoke. They looked at all the bushes and flowers that Margie had planted over the summer.

"The yard looks so beautiful and colorful this year, Margie. You did a great job with all the plants. I think I might get my easel out here and paint this," he said.

"That's a great idea. We can look at it over the fireplace when it's cold and snowy," she said.

"All the colors will keep us warm."

They finished their coffee and cigarettes and got Max's leash. Margie stayed to clean up, and MacDonald took Max for his walk. While walking, all he could think about was the case. He knew what the results of the forensics would show. All the evidence was pointing in one direction. With the new information he received from his officer and Father Michael, the puzzle was beginning to come together.

This is the way he figured it. Minnie and Father Don had some kind of altercation in the hallway that continued in the tub room. Minnie had the knife in her pocket. Maybe she brought it to work to open boxes or packages that the medications came in. He knew it could be for any reason.

The inscription said "Nova Scotia" on the handle. Minnie had been to Nova Scotia over her vacation this past summer. There were oxycodone pills scattered on the floor. This could have resulted from some sort of struggle. Father Don must have known what she was doing and was trying to talk to her.

Maybe he was going to expose her to Father Michael. She was very involved in her position, and with her erratic behavior, anything could have been misinterpreted. She was afraid someone would find out she was stealing narcotics from the residents. Why wasn't Tom Darcy there that morning? Did Minnie set up the scene so he would not be there? He would be the only witness to her crime.

Minnie was a big woman and very strong from all her weight lifting. She could have easily snuck up on him while his back was turned. Things were making sense now to Detective MacDonald.

He returned from his walk. As he entered the kitchen, Margie called him over for a phone call.

She cupped the receiver and said, "The forensic lab is on the phone. They want to speak with you."

He finished talking on the phone and hung up the receiver.

"I'm going to go downtown for about an hour, Margie. I'll be back," he said.

"OK, don't be too late. We don't want to miss the new season of *Bar Rescue*."

He then left to go to the precinct.

CHAPTER 34

EVERYONE AT THE Mansard House was glad that the state surveyors had come and left so quickly. Only minor recommendations were requested; otherwise it was a deficiency-free survey. Lilian and Jenn were having their usual lunch together in the cafeteria and things were settling back to normal.

"Henry is sponsoring a meeting of AA tonight in the auditorium. Father Michael said he could use the space. I think Father may attend, just to get the gist of the meeting," Jenn said.

"I don't think it would hurt him to hear what people have to say. He seems to drink quite a bit. He thinks no one knows it, but you can smell it on his breath," Lilian said.

"Well, I'm sure it's his way of dealing with everything that has been happening here in the past six months, don't you think so, Lilian?" she asked

"Absolutely. Not only is he dealing with Father Don's murder, he lost his director of nurses and had to deal with her addiction, not to mention the stress he's under as an administrator. There is talk through the grapevine that Minnie had something to do with Father Don's murder. Father Pat was let go, as he threatened Father Michael to get money to pay off his gambling debt. What else can go wrong? The poor man. His blood pressure must be skyrocketing," Lilian said.

"The man's a saint. I've never seen anyone follow the principles of Saint Francis of Assisi like he does. He's so kind and forgiving," Jenn said.

Just then the other employees were coming down for their lunch break. Steve, the new director of nurses, was eating his lunch with Dawn today. They seemed to be hitting it off great.

Dawn was very responsible and ethical and took her responsibility of caring for the elderly very serious.

"They found a knife in the pot up on the roof deck," Jenn said.

"I heard about that. Apparently it was Minnie's. She showed that to me when she came back from Nova Scotia," Lilian answered.

"She always had it in her pocket as a box cutter. There was always something to cut open with all the packaging on things."

Lilian did not want to gossip about Minnie. She still felt very bad about Minnie's situation. They were friends. Whatever happened, Lilian would be there to support her.

You don't turn your back on friends when they are down, she thought.

Ziggy had pretty much moved on.

"I heard she was working at a nursing home in Chelsea. She's attending UMass for nursing in the fall," Jenn chimed in.

"Good for her. She deserves some happiness in her life, with all she has been through," Lilian replied.

They finished up their lunch just as the cafeteria was filling up with other employees taking their lunch break.

"I'm heading upstairs to Mansard six. I have to check on one of the residents. He has a fever. Something's brewing," Lilian said.

"I'll catch you later, Lilian," Jenn replied.

On Mansard 6 the nurse that worked the evening shift with Minnie the morning Father Don was murdered was there.

"How is Mr. O'Neill?" Lilian asked

"He has a fever and seems a little delirious," she said.

Lilian went in to see him. He was burning up.

"Let's give him some acetaminophen to get his temperature down. His breathing sounds shallow, and I can hear wheezing on his left side. I think he may have pneumonia. Let's send him out. He needs IVs, he's dry," she said.

The nurse on the floor called the hospital and an ambulance was called to transport him. Lilian had a feeling he had the flu. She would know soon enough.

Sure enough the next day, the lab results were called back to Mansard 6. He had the flu. The whole floor was quarantined and the dining room closed. They wanted to contain it as much as possible. Too bad that didn't happen. Three more residents tested positive for flu.

Lilian was talking to the nurse who was working with Minnie the morning Father Don was murdered. She asked her if Minnie left the floor.

"Well, she went somewhere, but she didn't go to the cafeteria. The detective already questioned me on that," she said. "She did make a call to Tom Darcy, though, right here at the desk at five o'clock."

"Why?" Lilian asked.

"She told him not to come in that morning because his father didn't sleep well and she gave him some medication to let him rest. She said she didn't want Tom to take the long trip from Plymouth if he wasn't able to talk with his father," she said. "She told him to come later, when he would be awake."

Lilian thought about that. So Minnie didn't want Tom around, but Father Don was there and Minnie was there. What did she do?

Lilian left the floor and went back to her office to write up her reports. She wanted to get some distance from the nagging thoughts she was thinking. Minnie was very strong and the weight-lifting exercises for the Parkinson's disease were giving her more stability. If Father Don knew something about her, or was going to reveal what he knew to Father Michael, she could have been threatened. Minnie was very possessive about her pain medication and would do just about anything to get it, Lilian thought. To think she made up that lie about Mr. Darcy being asleep so that Tom would not come in, that's premeditation. Addiction was making her do these things. It just didn't seem possible that Minnie would put her career in jeopardy and become so violent that she would hurt someone. Lilian put all these suspicions out of her mind and put on her headphones. She turned on the radio 106.9 FM soft rock, to tune out her thoughts.

CHAPTER 35

ETECTIVE MACDONALD RECEIVED the results of the forensic testing on the knife.

The test results for Father Don's DNA came back positive, as well as Minnie McCracken's. Her fingerprints were all over the knife and the towel found at the scene of the crime.

All this evidence placed Minnie at the scene of the crime. Now all Detective MacDonald needed to do was get her to confess. She was a hard nut to crack and with her drug problem, volatile.

He knew Minnie would not let him back into her apartment without a search warrant, but maybe someone else could go in. He knew Minnie would not confess to him personally, but she might confess to someone else. The person she trusted most was Lilian.

He wondered if she would be willing to wear a wire. He knew Lilian was as anxious as everyone else to have this murder solved. So much had happened in six months' time.

In the meantime, back at the precinct, he was getting a search warrant ready to search Minnie's house. There could be some evidence there that would be conclusive. He made a call to Lilian at the Mansard House. He explained to her his plan and asked if she would help.

"It might solve the crime," he said.

Detective MacDonald planned to wire Lilian and have her ask specific questions. If things got out of hand, he would be right outside with Officer Ed and the police, if anything should happen.

That evening Lilian agreed to go and visit Minnie to check up on her. Lilian called, but there was no answer. She and Detective MacDonald would do it another night when Minnie was at home.

Back at the rectory, Father Michael was getting ready to visit the graveside of Father Don. The memorial Mass was coming up soon, and he needed to go there to see if any thoughts came to him. *What can one say? The deceased is still in our prayers and thoughts.*

That was part of it. Father Michael vowed to find his murderer and do anything he could to let Father Don rest in peace. He was facing old age alone without his good friend. It was all so senseless.

He had a lot of years ahead of him. To be struck down in the middle of his life was a sin.

Father Michael could not forgive the person who did this and thought he might never be able to.

While he was visiting at the grave, he heard someone approaching from behind. He turned and saw it was Ziggy with her little boy, Sami. Father Michael gave her a hug.

"He's getting big," he said.

"I'm so glad I ran into you," Ziggy said.

"Do you come here often?" Father Michael inquired.

"Almost weekly," she said. "See those flowers over there? I planted them a while ago. They are still blooming. Just like Father Don, who is still blooming in our hearts. I bring my Sami over to see his father. Someday when he is older he will ask me more about his life and I will tell him his father was a great man. He helped a lot of people, and especially me, to start a new life in America. It's sad to come here, but happy at the same time. He can see how his son is growing," she said.

"Father, I have something to ask you. I want to know where the siblings of Father Don live. I want them to know about their nephew. He's beginning to look like him, and I thought it would be a comfort for the family to see Sami."

"And add to that a shock as well," said Father Michael. "Let me call his brother and tell him the situation, and we will schedule a time for the family to come by. They can come to the rectory. Remember, they didn't know Father Don's plans to leave the priesthood or the fact he had a child. I'm sure they will be happy to meet Sami," he said. "It might be a shock at first, but they will welcome you, trust me." Then he asked, "How did you get over here from Chelsea?"

"My friend from back home gave me a ride. He's been here for a short time," she said.

Ziggy walked to the car and introduced Father Michael to Daniel.

"He's studying to be a pharmacist in this country," she said.

"Good for you. It's nice to meet you, Daniel."

"It's nice to meet you, Father," he replied.

Ziggy bid her farewell to Father Michael and got in the car. She and Daniel sat for a while talking and then drove off. Father Michael was happy for Ziggy. He could see in the young man's eyes that he cared for her. He wasn't worried about Ziggy anymore and knew it was her time to move on.

Seeing Father Don's son had a healing effect on him. He even looked like him. The sparkle in his eye and the smile were familiar. He hoped Ziggy would find some peace and happiness in her life now.

CHAPTER 36

CRYSTAL ATTENDED THE arraignment of her brother, Tom. All of the charges were read against him. His attorney pleaded not guilty. Crystal went by herself. John didn't know she was there.

She still cared for Tom. After all, he was her brother, her blood. Their parents were gone. Who did he have? His own wife never came. She had an order of protection against him. Crystal felt that money from the will drove him to this. That's not the Tom she knew. She wasn't sure if she would ever feel safe around him again. Once he was in jail, maybe then she would visit. *Let him think about what he did*, she thought. In the meantime Crystal was continuing to work part-time and was attending the Culinary Institute. She was thinking about her wedding date next summer and was waiting for John to have some free time to look at the venues. A wedding was a big production, and Crystal loved every minute of it. She felt sad that her mom was not around to help her with picking out the wedding dress and the food.

Her aunt Jane was stepping in for her mother and Crystal was so thrilled she was. She had an appointment at the Palace Room in Quincy and felt the location would be perfect for both families. Her extended family was from the South Shore and his family was from the North Shore. It would be perfect for everyone. They were planning to be married in the outdoor gazebo. Father Michael had already agreed to officiate at the ceremony. Both Crystal and John were Catholics and wanted a priest to give the blessing.

Tom had no idea that they were getting married, and he didn't need to know. In due time, she would tell him. Crystal planned on selling her father's home as it held too many sad memories for her now. They both wanted to buy a house that was newer or have one built. Crystal felt she wanted to move away from Milton and try living closer to John's family in Wilmington, Massachusetts.

She had already met most of his family and was particularly fond of his mother. She was very down to earth and so happy for them both. Crystal wanted to include her in as much of the wedding planning as possible. John had three brothers that would all be in the wedding. Since her father's passing, she always thought her brother would be the one to walk her down the aisle, but that wasn't realistic and she knew it. She and John had talked about it, and Crystal felt her father's younger brother would be perfect. Her uncle agreed to give her away. With all the drama that had happened over the past six months, Crystal was more than ready to move on to a new life. Things were stabilizing for her, and John was her main stabilizer. The money from her inheritance was being used for the wedding. Father Michael finally received the donation that was left to the Mansard House and the order.. Father Michael used part of it to purchase the property on L Street for the assisted living home. Some part of it was being used to renovate the Mansard House and to add a daycare on the first floor for the staff. A lot of the younger therapists and nursing staff were having babies, and a new daycare would help with keeping staff. Also, they were building an additional parking lot near the new house that staff could use to take a shuttle to work.

Father Michael also planned on buying a new car for the rectory, as his old Volkswagen had quite a few miles on it. With all the traveling they did, he purchased a brand new SUV all-wheel drive vehicle that would allow the priests to travel together. Some of the money was left to St George's Parish and the new monsignor there had planned to build a homeless shelter and a walk-in treatment clinic. This was Father Don's desire, and Father Michael was happy to fulfill it.

The six-month memorial Mass was coming up this Saturday, and Father was preparing himself for an emotional event. As much as people said that time would heal his grief, he knew it would just become part of his life. He was attending grief services that helped him cope with Father Don's death and planned on inviting Ziggy if she wanted to attend.

The investigation was lasting a long time and Father wondered if Detective MacDonald would ever solve the case. There were so many leads and wild goose chases that he felt maybe they would never know. Detective MacDonald shared with him his concerns regarding Minnie's involvement, but Father Michael did not even want to consider the possibility. He hoped it wasn't so.

CHAPTER 37

L ILIAN HAD ARRIVED at work early Friday morning. She called Detective MacDonald and reviewed with him the plan to visit Minnie and the wire she would be wearing.

She did not feel too comfortable doing this, but Detective MacDonald convinced her it was the only way. Minnie only trusted Lilian. She finished up her work early and explained to her husband the situation. He was a little concerned.

"What if something goes wrong? You could get hurt," he said.

"Minnie's in a bad situation. She needs help, and if she did murder Father Don, I want to help in any way I can. Besides, the detective and Officer Ed will be right outside as well the police. They just want Minnie to confess what she did."

After leaving work Lilian picked up a pizza and some soda to bring to Minnie's house. She arrived there around four o'clock in the afternoon. She rang the doorbell, and Minnie answered and let her in.

She seemed like she was feeling OK. Lilian noticed a little bit of a tremor.

"How's everything going, Minnie? How are you feeling?" she asked.

"I'm doing OK," she said. "I feel a little agitated because the rehab clinic will not refill my prescriptions and I need the pain medication."

"Minnie, aren't you taking the acetaminophen?" Lilian asked

"That doesn't do anything. I'm out of oxycodone, and the doctor won't write me a prescription for it."

"Minnie, you are not supposed to get it refilled. You are in the rehab to withdraw from it."

"Oh, that. I dropped out. I didn't want to continue, it wasn't helping," Minnie explained.

"What about the courts? I thought it was court-ordered rehab," she said.

"No, my attorney agreed that he would recommend that I attend rehab, but it wasn't a court order," she said.

"Well, what's the good of that? Now you are just not dealing with the problem," Lilian said.

"I have too many things on my mind," she said.

"Minnie, let's sit down and eat the pizza before it gets cold." They brought the food into the kitchen and began to eat. While enjoying the pizza, Lilian casually asked Minnie about that morning again, the day of the murder. Minnie was comfortable telling her the exact same story she told her before, only this time Lilian asked if she called Tom Darcy that morning and told him not to visit his father.

"Yes, I did. How did you know that?" Minnie asked

"I talked to the nurse on duty with you that morning," she said.

"Are you spying on me, Lilian? I think you have been listening to Detective MacDonald too much," Minnie said.

"No, Minnie, I just wanted to know if that was true."

"Yes, it was true. Mr. Darcy was up half the night. I didn't think it was fair for Tom to drive all the way up from Plymouth when his father would be sound asleep," she said

"Was Father Don there that morning? Did he say anything to you?" Lilian asked.

"You know he was a do gooder. He had that clinic in Dorchester for recovering addicts, and he was telling me about it. I don't know why he was telling me. We had a few words about it, and then we stepped into the tub room to talk privately."

"What did you talk about?" she asked.

"Apparently, Father Michael told him about my problem with taking pain pills, and he felt it was his place to counsel me about it. I told him my personal business was none of his business, and he seemed to back off. He then asked me if I had any medication on me. I showed him the prescription bottle that I had for oxycodone, written by my doctor. He tried to take it away from me. We had a little struggle, and I got the pills back," Minnie said.

Lilian was shocked at what Minnie was telling her. She needed to tread lightly as not to upset her.

"Minnie, did you stab Father Don?" she asked.

Minnie slowly turned to get her pocketbook on the chair behind her. She reached in and took out a small-caliber pistol, turned around, and pointed it straight at Lilian.

"Minnie, what are you doing?" she said with a quiver in her voice.

"I did, Lilian. He tried to take my medication. He grabbed the bottle from me and planned on telling Father Michael about this incident. He threatened to call the board of nursing to have my license revoked. Could you imagine—all the years I put into my career, and he was threatening to expose me?"

Lilian just stood there dumbfounded.

"I want you to take out your prescription pad and write me a prescription for oxycodone, and do it now," Minnie said while pointing the gun at her.

"Minnie, you know I can't do that. What about my license? You're a known drug abuser."

"I don't care," Minnie screamed at her. "You will do it. Don't make me lose my temper, Lilian!!"

Lilian looked at her.

"Is that what happened to Father Don? You lost your temper?" she said.

"That's exactly what happened, Lilian. I didn't mean to do it. I had the knife in my hand, we struggled, and I stabbed him. I had to get my pills. I didn't plan it, like you're thinking, it just happened."

Just then the back door flew open. Lilian ducked under the table and hit the floor. Minnie was still standing with the pistol pointing where she had been sitting a moment ago. Ed fired a warning shot in the air and commanded her to drop the gun and place her hands over her head.

Minnie seemed to be in a trance. In the next instant, Detective MacDonald stormed in the front door and startled her, while Officer Ed twisted her arm till the gun fell to the floor.

The police entered the house and handcuffed Minnie. "We have a warrant for your arrest for the murder of Father Donald O'Sullivan. You are being taken into custody." The police officer escorted her out to the patrol car as he was reading her Miranda rights.

Lilian got up from under the table. Her husband, James, came running in; he had been outside listening in on the receiver as the whole scene unfolded. He knew Detective MacDonald from seeing him in court and called him that morning. He didn't want anything to happen to Lilian, and he rushed in to help her up off the floor.

"Are you all right, Lilian?" he yelled.

"I'm OK, James, just shocked and a little shaken up," she said.

James put his arm around her shoulder and escorted her out of the house.

The next day, the news of Minnie's arrest and involvement in the murder was all over the airwaves. Father Michael couldn't believe it. He didn't know what to think. He was relieved that Father Don's murderer was apprehended, but he was sad about the whole situation.

Minnie needed help, and she needed a good attorney.

Lilian called Father Michael because she had decided to give her resignation. She had enough excitement for one year. She planned on taking a position at Mercy Hospital in Cambridge, but not before she took some time off to spend with her family.

Father Pat in Yonkers heard the news on Channel 9. *Well, I'll be dammed! Who would have ever thought it was Minnie?* He shook his head back and forth as the news continued. Jenn heard the news on the radio. She could not believe Minnie would do such a thing.

Ziggy was at work at the nursing home in Chelsea. She was feeding one of the residents his breakfast when she saw on the news pictures of the arrest and Minnie being taken into custody.

She moved over to the television to increase the volume.

The anchorwoman said Minnie McCracken was apprehended last night at her home after pointing a gun at her coworker. No one was hurt. The suspect was placed in handcuffs and taken into custody for the murder of Father Donald O'Sullivan. The investigation into his murder had lasted six months.

Bail was currently being set.

Ziggy sat on the chair silently for a moment. She placed her hands over her face and made the sign of the cross. *Thank you, Lord. My prayers have been answered. Now*, she thought, *he can rest in peace.*

The End

AUTHOR BIO

Jane Mengesha grew up in Dorchester, Massachusetts. She graduated from Framingham State College and has worked in the Nursing Home industry for over 25 years.

She is the mother of five children and lives in the greater Boston area with her family.

This is her first novel.

AUTHORS NOTE

I would like to thank my sister Louise Mackin and my friend, Laura McNamara for reviewing my manuscript.

I would also like to thank my husband Haile and my children Sarah, Elizabeth, Michael, Lilian and Joseph for their advice, support and patience while I was writing this novel.

Special thanks to all my friends and family who read my murder mystery.

Jane Mengesha